WHO WANTS TO BE A SUPERHERO IF YOU CAN BE A BUSINESS COACH?

THE CORRECT AND SUCCESSFUL WAY TO BE A BUSINESS COACH

ELVIN COACHES

© **Copyright 2020 - All rights reserved.**

The content contained within this book may not be reproduced, duplicated or transmitted without direct written permission from the author or the publisher.

Under no circumstances will any blame or legal responsibility be held against the publisher, or author, for any damages, reparation, or monetary loss due to the information contained within this book, either directly or indirectly.

Legal Notice:

This book is copyright protected. It is only for personal use. You cannot amend, distribute, sell, use, quote or paraphrase any part, or the content within this book, without the consent of the author or publisher.

Disclaimer Notice:

Please note the information contained within this document is for educational and entertainment purposes only. All effort has been executed to present accurate, up to date, reliable, complete information. No warranties of any kind are declared or implied. Readers acknowledge that the author is not engaged in the rendering of legal, financial, medical or professional advice. The content within this book has been derived from various sources. Please consult a licensed professional before attempting any techniques outlined in this book.

By reading this document, the reader agrees that under no circumstances is the author responsible for any losses, direct or indirect, that are incurred as a result of the use of the information contained within this document, including, but not limited to, errors, omissions, or inaccuracies.

CONTENTS

Introduction   7

1. BUSINESS COACHING ON THE HIGHEST LEVEL   13
   What Can a Coach Really Do?   17
   Why You'll Love Being a Business Coach   23
   How to Become a Business Coach   26

2. THE ESSENCE OF BUSINESS COACHING CREDIBILITY   36
   How to Build Credibility   38
   What to Avoid as a Coach   44
   Why Vulnerability is Important   48
   Help Your Client Become Vulnerable   53
   The Importance of Privacy   57

3. TIME MANAGEMENT TIPS TO INCREASE PRODUCTIVITY   58
   Time Management Coach Strategies   59
   Why Procrastination is Bad   64
   How to Build a Habit   68
   Time in Terms of Philosophy   72
   Manage Your Time   74
   Who Are Your Prospective Clients?   79
   Steps to Increase Productivity   82

4. MARKETING COACHING   85
   Who Is a Marketing Coach?   86
   Why Do Businesses Hire a Marketing Coach?   90

Specific Marketing Strategies	94
Complementing With a Blog	97
5. COMMON BUSINESS COACHING QUESTIONS	**101**
Dissecting the Grow Model	103
Questioning Techniques	110
6. TOP CORE BUSINESS COACHING SKILLS	**116**
Coaching Skills	117
Increasing Empathy	130
7. LEADERSHIP DEVELOPMENT COACH	**134**
Leadership Development Coaching	136
Benefits of Leadership Development Coaching	137
Skills Needed for Leadership Development Coaching	139
Principles of Leadership Development Coaching	143
Why Hire a Leadership Development Coach	145
Business/Life Balance	146
Conclusion	151
References	159

Just for you!

Scan the QR code to subscribe or follow the link
https://elvinlifecoaches.activehosted.com/f/3

A FREE GIFT TO OUR READERS

You're going to receive the

Wheel of Life Coaching Technique

and other goodies

INTRODUCTION

Imagine a young and ambitious adult who recently graduated from college. She received her degree in engineering and was hired by a major firm in her city. While the job paid well and her prospects were good, after a couple of years, she grew tired of being someone's employee. Most of all, she was getting tired of engineering. While in high school, she had dreams of starting a business, but the influential adults around her advised against it. It was too risky to start a business from scratch and they encouraged her to follow a safer path. As a result, she studied civil engineering in college and got a job in this field instead.

During college, she never developed a true passion for engineering even though she was amazing at math. After being with her employer for a couple of years, she was burned out and ready for something else. Unlike in high school, she was independent now and able to make more of her own decisions. Her goal now was to open a food truck and travel around town making unique meals. She was excited about this new change. However, she has no idea how to get started.

She does not want to ask any family members because they will only discourage her. She also does not know who else to turn to for solid advice. As a result, she is ready to give up on her dreams already. The stress, isolation, and fear of failure are not worth it.

In a situation like this, this young professional will benefit greatly from a business coach. Business coaching is a fascinating field where people get individual guidance in creating and developing their business ideas. A business coach has the ability to keep you on a directed path so that you make the best decisions in relation to your venture, whether they are financial, industry-related, marketing, or a wealth of other factors.

A business coach will never tell you what to do but will help you find the best answers within yourself. We all know ourselves best and sometimes it takes an objective viewpoint to understand which direction we must go. A business coach is a perfect individual for this.

Whether you are thinking about starting a business, are in the initiation phase, or have been running your business for a while, you will be struggling in many ways. There are many answers out there and it's difficult to determine what the ideal path is. The fear of starting a business and having it fail is very common. No matter how long a business has been running, the market is always changing, and the risk of losing everything always exists. A business coach can guide you in making sure this does not happen. They will help you come up with solutions based on your unique problems and also hold you accountable. The best part is, you will never feel like you are alone like so many business owners do.

As you go through the chapters of this book, you will gain a detailed understanding of what a business coach is and how they can help you as a business owner and entrepreneur. You will understand the many strategies and techniques that will guide you in becoming a successful business owner and not a statistic that is on the road to failure. In addition, we will discuss the many questions and information a business coach will have for you, so you can have an idea of how the process works. Asking the right questions at the right time and with the right demeanor is one of the foundations of good business coaching. Finally, we will go over some of the subspecialties within the business coaching umbrella.

Not only will you understand the process of working with a business coach, but whether or not you want to become one yourself. Since we are a part of the industry and recognize the many benefits it provides, we like to encourage other passionate people to join the field. Once you have read this book and realize how effective the practice is, there's a good chance you will want to join the coaching profession and assist others in the same manner. We are here to help you on your new journey.

Business

WHO ARE WE?

We are part of a collective known as Elvin Coaches. We have several members and decades of experience between all of us. We all met in Indonesia years ago and many of us were already practicing life coaches by then. This became a huge bonding moment between us and we have all grown as a family since then, supporting each other every step of the way.

We have all personally experienced the power that all forms of coaching has, both for the client and the coach. We learn from the people we help just as much as they learn from us.

All of us at Elvin Coaches are passionate about what we do that we wanted to get our knowledge and experience out to the masses. This is why we wrote this book as part of our series. We feel it is the best way for us to impart our knowledge to many people around the world. Whether you need the help of a business coach or want to become one yourself, we are here to help you. We want to make you a part of our family. Once you are, you will grow exponentially as a person through our step-by-step action plans we provide and be able to guide others to do the same.

(Fauxels, n.d.-b)

1

BUSINESS COACHING ON THE HIGHEST LEVEL

Business coaching is a subset of the broader art of life coaching. While life coaches generally assist clients in every area of their lives, business coaches are geared towards guiding clients in planning, initiating, and running a business. This includes helping them find answers to overcome real and potential threats to their business model.

Whether you are running a major corporation, a small business in your neighborhood, or work as an entrepreneur from home, there are specific challenges that come your way which you must be able to anticipate. These challenges might be common for all business owners, or unique to your industry or situation. The bottom line is, you will struggle immensely as a business owner through every process and the bigger your company becomes, the more potential problems there will be.

There is a lot of confusion out there about the difference between business coaching and consulting. The main separating factor is that a consultant will do the work for your business while the coach is more like a guiding presence who gives you the knowledge, training, tools, and guidance to do it yourself. For those wondering why it's more worthwhile to hire someone who will show you how to do it yourself versus someone who will do it themselves, the answer simply is that the business belongs to you.

As a business owner, in whatever capacity that might be, you must understand on your own what the best way to run and grow the business is. In the long run, it will be your responsibility and the issue with hiring a consultant is that once they are gone, all of the old problems related to past methods will return. When you hire a coach, you will do the work by finding the answers within yourself. Why is this better? Once again, it is your business and you are the one ultimately responsible for its success.

Think about the example of going to the gym and hiring a personal trainer. Why would you hire a trainer at the gym and pay them when you can just go in and start working out? Well, even if you use all of the equipment and go hard, you can still get zero to minimal results. You may not lose any weight or build any muscle. The trainer can help guide you by giving you exercises to target certain muscle groups and also provide instructions on meal planning. While the trainer will guide you,

you are responsible for doing the work. Unfortunately, we cannot become fit by other people exercising. At least, not just yet.

This idea holds true for hiring a business coach to help you with your business practices. You can just go in and start doing everything yourself, but that does not mean you will do it right. You could end up making massive mistakes that should have been avoided, but you were woefully unaware because you are not experienced in the business. Even if you are experienced, having an objective third party to give you instructions on maintaining the right path will still be helpful. Just like with a trainer, a business coach can help you with focus and targeted actions to minimize mistakes and bring in tremendous results, but they cannot and will not do the work for you.

The information, ideas, and skills you pick up from working with a business coach will last you a lifetime. So, even if the coach is gone, you can still succeed because you will have the answers within you. The following is a quick rundown of the many things a business coach can help you with:

- Setting better goals that are geared towards business growth.
- Coming up with action steps to reach said goals.
- Reaching goals at a faster rate.
- Making appropriate decisions that will lead to business growth.

- Improving relationships with customers, clients, partners, employees, and anyone else involved with the business.

Business coaching is not about what you have done in the past. That was an experience that you learned from. It is really about the future and the potential you can create for your organization. As coaching to over 100 clients over the years, we understand how valuable coaching can be to help owners achieve their goals.

As a business owner, you work for yourself and there is no one to motivate you except for yourself. There is no boss or predetermined deadlines. You do all of this yourself. Many individuals have a hard time finding the discipline or motivation to keep moving and stay on top of everything. Many people have no idea if they should do everything themselves or hire help. If they hire help, what kind of help will it be and how can they afford it on a shoestring budget? What programs exist to make business practices smoother? How can I reach my customer base? There are so many questions out there that business owners have and a business coach can help answer most, if not all of them.

Most of all, a business coach can hold you accountable. Most individuals work harder and do what they are supposed to do if they know someone is watching over them. Going back to the gym example, many patrons who go to workout simply do it lazily with little effort. On many occasions, they are spending more time on their phones and barely putting anything into their routines. Furthermore, they are only targeting specific areas on their bodies and completely ignoring others. A trainer can help gym-goers massively improve their workouts and outcomes, and business coaches can help you, as a business owner, do the same.

WHAT CAN A COACH REALLY DO?

To drive the point home about business coaches, we want to give you an in-depth perspective on what they can really do. As you have read this chapter so far, you are probably wondering why you can't just read a business book, attend a seminar, talk to a business owner, get a consultation, or speak to friends and family members. Why do you need to pay someone to tell you something you can learn for free? This last question can be debunked immediately because what a coach is able to tell you cannot be learned for free from anybody. If someone is actually helping you plan and personalize your path as a business owner to the extent a coach does and they are doing it for free, then they must really like you.

The truth is, all of the above options are beneficial to a degree. You can learn a lot from reading a book or talking to a business owner, but the personal guidance you will receive from any of these choices will be severely limited. For example, a business owner can give you advice, but maybe not personal advice specifically geared towards your business. A book or seminar will not be by your side to help you during unexpected moments. Friends and family might mean well, but they are often biased in their approach if they don't have the depth or breadth of knowledge necessary to properly advise.

A business coach will work as an objective third party who can give personal guidance at any point of business progression. They will be there to encourage you, but also hold your feet to the fire. When challenges arise, a coach will help you assess the situation and come up with the best answers for yourself. People who hire business coaches take a lot of solace in knowing they are not alone in their venture. Unfortunately, many business owners do feel this way, which is a shame. This is why it's important to recognize how useful business coaching can be.

So many startups fail before they even have a chance to get going. It's sad to think about the many amazing products or services that did not make it in this world because an individual did not know how to take it off the ground. They wanted to succeed but couldn't get past the barriers. It's time to start changing that. Business and entrepreneurship give you more potential for success than you could ever have dreamed possible. With all of the uncertainty of the world and job market, the ability to start a business has never been more attractive. The opportunities are endless as long as you know what you're doing. With a business coach, always knowing what to do next becomes much easier and less frightening.

One thing to understand is that coaches do not teach practical business skills. They will work more like a silent partner who is helping to hold you up. They will support your growth whether you are just starting, think about starting, or are highly experienced. Even successful business owners need coaches. You never know when bad decisions can cause a dramatic shift and a coach can help avoid things like this from happening.

Provide an Outside Perspective

The first thing a business coach can do is look at your situation as an outside observer with zero bias involved. From here, they can help you determine what is and isn't working for you and why. A good coach will help you recognize what your role is within the business and how it can align with your personal life in regards to your talents, core values, and vision.

An outside observer like a coach can also help determine where and when you are getting in your own way. Moments like these stunt the growth of your business and the more you can eliminate them, the better it will be for your progress.

Helps Establish Vision and Goals

Coaches help business owners set up the right individual vision and goals. It is crucial in any business to develop long-term goals that work well with what you're seeking in life. Having arbitrary symbols of success that don't relate to you in any way will not work in the long run. A coach helps align goals with people's values.

Coaches can uncover underlying inspiration for wanting success in business. Some examples include:

- Making a positve impact on the world.
- Having more autonomy to live a life that you want.
- Personal fulfillment and helping others solve a major problem.
- Creating jobs for people.
- Building wealth and leaving a legacy for your family.

Basically, a coach will help their clients figure out their "why" for starting a business. Whether a business is just a dream or a full-fledged organization, the "why" will always be important. If you don't know yours, then you are in danger of burning out and losing control.

A business coach will help you figure out your vision first and your goal second. This way, your business will follow what you truly value in life. If you are feeling directionless, getting help from an experienced coach can do wonders for you.

Goals!

Work With a Person's Strengths and Weaknesses

Everyone has their strengths and weaknesses, and that's okay. The problem occurs when people don't recognize where they are weak or if they don't take advantage of their strengths. A business coach can hold up a proverbial mirror so you can see these strengths and note the skills that you need to improve upon.

Building on strengths is a major shortcut to success. Being overly focused on what we're not good at, as many people are, can easily distract us from what we are already doing well. Coaches use a number of tools to determine how you learn, work, and relate to others. They will pick out areas where you shine and help you maximize these gifts to their full potential.

It's important to manage weaknesses, even if we can't turn them into strengths. The best thing to do here is to figure out how to not get tripped up by weaknesses to the point they halt your progress. Business coaches will help you discover the blind spots that are holding you back and then guide you towards growth, making your weaknesses ineffective.

Provide Accountability

Accountability is one of the most essential reasons for having a coach. It is easy to become lazy, not follow up on things, and take massive shortcuts. If we don't get caught, then what's the big deal? Well, if you're trying to run and build a business, then there's plenty that can go wrong. Not being held accountable can result in you going down the wrong direction. Business ownership is rewarding, but a long and arduous process every step of the way. During good and bad times, it is easy to lose sight of things and revert back to old habits or develop new bad habits. Luckily, a coach will help keep you on the right track and let you know when you're faltering.

Hiring a business coach is a sound investment that can significantly increase your potential and grow your business as you see fit. If you're still wondering how beneficial coaching can be, here are some questions to ask yourself:

- Do you want to work with someone who will challenge your thought process and make you think more deeply about yourself?
- Will it be helpful to have someone use intuitive tools and innovative practices to learn more about your business and what it needs? More importantly, what you need?
- Does the idea of maximizing your full potential get you excited?
- Are you willing to take responsibility for what you need to do?
- Remember that coaching is a collaborative practice where both parties involved do their part. The coach guides while the client listens and takes action.
- Are you ready to work and improve yourself by putting in the work every day?

If you answered yes to these questions, even just a few of them, then you are ready to enter the realm of business coaching. After working with a coach, you will have a new perspective on many facets of your business. You will finally be creating the type of life you deserve. If you like what you have read so far, you might be ready to become a business coach yourself.

WHY YOU'LL LOVE BEING A BUSINESS COACH

Life coaching is a great career to get into. Not only will you help people, but you will also learn more about yourself. Business coaching is one of the categories under the life coach umbrella. Business coaches can help those who are in some of their worst financial states to completely turn their lives around. Before discussing how to become a business coach, we will go over some of the advantages it provides.

You Double Your Rate of Personal Development

Becoming a coach and then practicing in the field will give you a two-for-one deal. As you become a coach, you will learn the strategies that help other businesses, and when you impart that knowledge on a client, you are learning again. Plus, you will learn about the diverse issues, some unique and unexpected, that your clients are going through. One of the best ways to learn something is to teach it.

As a coach, you are not required to be an expert on everything. In fact, there will be times you will know very little about the industry your client is involved in. That's okay because the techniques used in coaching will work across the spectrum. So, while you have to be well-versed in those techniques, you do not have to know everything about your client's business.

Make an Extraordinary Living

While money is not the main driving force behind coaching, once you become good at your craft, you will be highly sought out. This will lead to significant financial gain. Some great coaches out there are making a six-figure income in a year while some of the top coaches are making millions. While it may take a while to reach this point, if you keep honing your craft and getting better, there is no reason why you can't reach this level someday. You will be helping people at the highest level.

Building Lasting and Empowering Relationships

You will get to know your clients on an intimate level and will continue working with them for years. You will even be able to hold special events with them. You might even build up professional networks.

You Become an Expert in Business

As you work with clients to develop mastery in their business, you will develop mastery in your own. In the process, you will be practicing the techniques that you are teaching.

As business coaches help their clients explore ways to gain success, they are discovering their own methods at the same time. The truth is, if this is not occurring, you need to step up your game in regards to your coaching skills. Clients will believe in you more if you are practicing what you preach. It does not get any simpler than that.

You Become Well-Positioned for the Next Opportunity

As a coach, you receive front-row education about some of the top business ventures in the world. When you work with experienced business owners and help them navigate through tough waters, you pick up a lot of great information as well. You are getting paid to gain both business experience and education. Because of this education, you get to evaluate some of the best ideas out there. As a result, you will be poised to take on some of the greatest opportunities that come about in the future.

You Get to Give Your Gift

As a coach, you will learn some amazing techniques and strategies that can change a person's life. This is truly a gift and you get to give this gift every single day. Many coaches are in their coaching mindset even if they are not working with a client. The knowledge you receive gives you a different mindset of how you see the world and solve problems. Therefore, you will be benefiting people with your practices even if they are not your client.

Most people who go to work adopt a different personality. The ways they conduct themselves are completely different at home and in their place of business. As a coach, you can just be yourself all the time. Whenever you are interacting with someone in your life, they are receiving your coaching persona which becomes natural.

One issue this can raise is when you are just having a conversation versus actually providing free coaching. As a business coach, you have a valuable skill that helps business owners in a tremendous way. You must make sure you are being compensated properly and not being taken advantage of.

You Will be Appreciated

As you help people move from mediocrity to excellence with their businesses, you will gain a lot of appreciation from your clients. They will see you as part of their process in gaining wealth and will value the skills you bring.

HOW TO BECOME A BUSINESS COACH

If you believe it is too soon to become a business coach after just learning about the practice, don't be too quick to dismiss yourself. Just like any other business, developing a coaching practice requires specific actions, knowledge, and training. If you are reading this book, then you probably were thinking about starting a business anyway. If coaching interests you, then why not take this path.

Many individuals want to become a phenomenal business coach, but do not believe they have the qualifications, whatever those may be. What if we told you that there aren't any official qualifications, you just need to have specific goals, mindsets, and the desire to make a difference in the world. You don't have to necessarily go to a four-year university or pick up multiple types of certifications [though getting some certification is recommended]. Is it an easy road? Definitely not. However, once you go down the path, you will understand how rewarding the practice can be.

When you are developing a coaching practice, you have the opportunity to immediately put into practice what you are advising your clients. As you are helping your clients, you are learning how to help yourself too.

Business coaches change lives. They help people realize their dreams of being successful business owners. They inspire people to become the best versions of themselves. Finally, they develop strong and secure bonds with their clients. When you help that struggling business owner or aspiring entrepreneur become who they were meant to be, it gives you one of the biggest highs in the world. This alone is enough to inspire someone to get into the field. If you find all of this exciting, then coaching might be right up your alley.

What does it take to become a successful business coach? Just like any form of life coaching, it is an unregulated profession, so there is no formal training. This means anyone can become a business coach, which can certainly have its positives and negatives. Of course, the more credential and experience you have, the more credible your clients will find you. We will discuss building credibility more in chapter two.

It takes a lot of time, effort, and sacrifice to become a great coach. It does not happen overnight. Even when you reach a level of greatness, there is always more to learn. Your growth as a coach will never stop.

You may never become the perfect coach because nobody ever does. Improvements are essential to address and take care of. One of the best ways to ensure you will do well is to approach the field with a proper mindset, which we will discuss right here.

The Right Mindset

Becoming a business coach requires a certain mindset. This will be one of the main deciding factors on whether you have lifelong success or will fizzle out quickly. Your destiny as a coach will be decided by how your mind works. If you have a poor mindset, then you will create poor results. The good news is, your mindset is something you can control. The problem is, many coaches, old and new, don't realize that their way of thinking could be causing them to fail. This is why we wanted to address this with you right away.

Having multiple years of coaching between all of us, Elvin Coaches believe in having a specific attitude when approaching the field of business coaching. The following are some of the traits you must develop if you are to enter the field of coaching and become successful.

Self-Belief

The bottom line is, if you do not believe in yourself, then no one else will believe in you either. Successful business coaches have 100% belief in their skills, products, and services and they are not afraid to share them. They know for a fact they can help others and in your quest to become a coach, you must feel the exact same way.

Lifelong Learner

Successful coaches ever stop learning because they know they are far from perfect, no matter how good they become. They are always looking for ways to improve their personal and professional growth and are willing to invest in their education. The best coaches are always on the lookout for courses, seminars, engagements, and even opportunities to get mentored. No matter how much you learn as a coach, never believe that you know it all.

Purposeful

They have a strong purpose behind what they do that goes well beyond making money. While you can certainly create a great income as a coach, just ask Tony Robbins or Brian Tracy, this should not be your ultimate purpose for becoming one. There needs to be a bigger "why" behind all of this. This can be helping someone realize their dreams or changing people's lives.

Accountable

Business coaches follow their own lead of holding others accountable by also holding themselves accountable. You must do this in order to get the results you desire and become focused on your goals and dreams.

Driven

Business coaches are driven to become the very best they can be at all times. They have a high level of ambition and are motivated to keep going. They are not afraid of hard work and doing what it takes to make it to the top.

Brave

All great coaches are brave enough to tell their clients what they need to hear and not what they want to hear. This is the essence of coaching because clients who are constantly praised for everything only get a bloated ego and don't have any real growth. Business coaches are not seeking praise. They genuinely want to help their clients and this can mean making them feel uncomfortable at times.

Service-Oriented

Business coaches are in the field of service. They enjoy helping as many people as they can and contributing in some way to their success. We can tell you from experience that watching someone turn their lives around because of the help you gave them as a coach produces a tremendous high.

Overall, business coaches need to be motivating, dedicated, helpful in setting up performance plans, and be very empowering. As a business owner as well as a coach, you will need to know when to delegate and manage your time appropriately. Items you can delegate can be things like marketing, website development, sending emails, or making phone calls, etc. Chapter three of this book will get heavy into time management.

As you can see, these mindset tactics are not exclusive to coaching. they can be utilized for success in any area of your life. To reach the highest level in any field, you must be fully committed.

Specializing

Once you have decided that to become a coach and understand the mindset that is involved, another factor to consider is the type of business coach you want to become. Business coaching is a subset of life coaching and from here there are many more categories to consider. You can certainly be a general business coach and help every type of business owner to a certain degree. On the other hand, you can become specialized and work with a niche group of people. This second option may give you the potential for more income, but a lot of that will have to do with marketing and how you present yourself.

Some examples of specializing include:

- Helping a specific age group like Millennials or Gen-Z, who are new to the business world.
- Working with single moms who want to become entrepreneurs.
- Working with online business owners.
- Coaching those who want to get into sales and marketing.

Working with a specific niche is a great way to get extra attention. You can start speaking to a specific group of people.

A Few More Steps

We will end this chapter by going over a few general steps on how you can get your coaching practice up and running. Remember, coaching is a passion, but you must also treat it like a business. That is the only way you will continue to get clients and keep your practice afloat. Here is a quick and easy guide to start your practice and build it to the next level:

Join a Network

A network is a group of people who are on a similar mission as you. In order to get your coaching business known, you can set up your own marketing campaigns, but you can also join various networking groups, including specific coach or business groups. Joining a group like this will introduce you to like-minded people and you guys can share your passion and promote each other's work in the community. You will also gain a lot of education by doing this.

Create a Business Plan

Starting a business without a plan is like building a house without a blueprint. You should never do it. A solid business plan will help you determine exactly what you need to do, how you will do it, how you will fund it, and how quickly you will get it done. The plan is not just for starting the business, but also running and growing it in the future. A business plan will give you complete clarity in how you will proceed with your coaching business. FYI, as a business coach, you may find yourself assisting many of your clients in creating their own business plan.

Make Sure You Have Capital

The good news is, coaching does not require a lot of capital compared to many other business ventures. However, you will still need some finances for marketing purposes and to live off of while you are developing your practice.

Secure Your Own Coach

While you are working on becoming a coach, secure your own business coach who can guide you along the way. Imagine the massive learning opportunities both of you will have.

Have a Solid Marketing Plan

If you start up a coaching practice but have no clue how you will get leads or find new clients, you are setting yourself up for failure. It does not matter how good of a coach you are, if people do not know you exist, then you will not be successful. Having a solid marketing plan is essential in this regard. Your marketing plan needs to clearly state what you do and who your target group, or niche, is, and how you are going to reach out to them. Marketing is one of the toughest and most important aspects of the business. It is how you get your clients.

Be Consistent

As a coach, you must remain consistent with what you do. For example, with marketing, you cannot jump around from one thing to another. You must focus on a few things to see if they work for you, or not. Once you have given the strategies an opportunity, then you can move on if needed. However, you must be consistent for long term success.

Always Improve

As a coach, you must always find ways to improve yourself. You must also keep up with new techniques and strategies that are beneficial for your clients and your practice. This is why it's important to read, attend seminars and workshops, and join networking groups.

Now that you understand what a business coach does and how to create a successful practice, we will get into more specific topics related to the field. By the end of the book, you will gain an in-depth idea of exactly what a business coach can do and how to be successful as one yourself.

(Juhaszimrus, n.d.)

2

THE ESSENCE OF BUSINESS COACHING CREDIBILITY

Trust

In any type of business you decide to get into, you need to find people to buy your product and/or service. This can take a lot of effort as there are so many moving parts. One of the things potential clients look for is credibility. Once again, this is not something that is built up overnight. The same holds true for business coaching. As a coach, you need to build up your credibility so that your clients will trust you enough to give you a chance. Remember, many of them will be in vulnerable states and they might be very cautious about who they can trust. When you have some credibility behind your name, the chances of clients seeking out your services will increase greatly. If you do a great job, your reputation will grow.

Unfortunately, many business owners forget about this aspect and end up jumping into the deep end of the pool right away. They begin creating outlandish coaching programs, running expensive marketing campaigns, and charging ridiculous prices for their services. These coaches are not in the profession to help people, they are here just to make money, and that's the wrong approach to take. Making money is an extra benefit that comes from being an excellent coach, but it should never be the main reason to go into the profession. It should not be your "why." If it is, your clients will see right through it and you will not have any credibility at all.

From the moment you start coaching on your first day, your focus needs to be on creating results for your client. They are coming to you because they need help with their business and your job is to be there for them to the best of your ability. Yes, marketing and putting yourself out there is important. However, when you help your business clients gain results, it will speak volumes for you. Your reputation will spread like wildfire through the mouths of the people you work with, so do your best to make sure they are speaking well of you.

HOW TO BUILD CREDIBILITY

As a business coach, you will be a mentor to your clients, and it is important to be credible in this regard to gain optimal success in the field. Your reputation, and therefore, your credibility, rests heavily on your clients trusting you. Even if you're acting like your authentic self with your clients, establishing credibility will be much more difficult than you think. Remember that your clients do not know you on a personal level. They may not know whether or not you're being honest with them. That's why it's important to do whatever you can to build up some trust.

Establishing trust early on will set the tone for the relationship you have with your clients and will give you something to build off of for the remainder of the time you are together. The question now is, how do we build trust and credibility with our clients? The focus of this chapter will be to discuss the most effective techniques for building a strong rapport with your coaching clients. Once you create this type of relationship, you will develop credibility in their eyes.

Build a Foundation

Create some social media accounts related to your coaching practice and, at least a couple of times a week, put out helpful content that potential clients will see and gain value from. These posts should be written for the sole purpose of engaging people and providing them helpful information. It should not have a sales tone to it. Your goal is to build a foundation with these posts so that people can see that you know what you're talking about. After reading these posts, business owners will be able to know exactly how you can help them. Think about your social media as a window into who you are. Every time you write anything on there, you are showing a part of yourself.

Stay on the Path

Establishing a voice and your brand is one of the hardest things to do in business. Having a consistent voice that views problems and solutions through a single lens can help establish a coach and client relationship. Your voice should express who you are because it will attract the clients that are meant to work with you. You will not be the right coach for everybody and that's okay. When you are working with the clients who will benefit from you, you will make a successful coach.

Gather Credentials

We already established that coaching is a largely unregulated profession, but that does not mean your clients will not be looking for credentials. Whether you like it or not, people are attracted to degrees and certifications that show some type of training. We are not asking you to get a college degree. However, getting some credentials is definitely a good idea. When you are a new coach, you will not have the benefit of reviews and people speaking highly of you. Getting some certifications can make you look more professional.

The International Coaching Federation or ICF is a good organization to go through. Furthermore, just because the coaching profession is not highly regulated now, it does not mean it won't be in the future. Some organizations are already asking for coaches to have certification. You might as well be ahead of the curve.

Teach From Experience

There are many experts, but not enough practitioners. People are more interested in your actions than they are your words. If you talk the talk but cannot walk the walk, then you will lose rapport with your clients in the end. If you want to establish credibility in the market, make sure you are living the way you teach others. If you are guiding your client and they can see that your actions match your words, they will view you as a credible coach who believes in what they are saying. Be a practitioner of your own teachings.

Be Real

Your clients are not looking for a fake persona. They are looking for you to be your unique self. When your clients start to see you as a real person who is also learning and living, they will start to trust and relate with you much more. Don't be afraid to speak from the heart and show them the real you. Don't divulge details of your life that neither you nor your client would be comfortable with. That's unprofessional. Just loosen up and give them a small taste of who you are.

Be Remarkably Different

People are not going to be attracted to you because you are a cookie-cutter version of everyone else. Being remarkably different and your own person will give you more credibility with your clients. To do this, you must determine your values, voice, and personal views. After this, create a unique value proposition for your clients. Clients want to be treated as individuals, and if you are showing that you're different from everyone else, it will assert some credibility for you in this regard. People will be more comfortable around you if they can see you are not just a carbon copy of other coaches.

Rave About Your Case Studies

As you serve more clients and help them benefit, your credibility will soar. Don't be afraid to let the public know how you helped people in the past. If some of your clients are willing to give you positive reviews, that's a good thing, as well.

Offer Value All the Time

Every time you are coaching a client, whether in person, over the phone, a video conference call, or simply emailing them some information, you must offer them value at all times. You must always strive to be at your best because it will build your credibility and it is not fair to your client if you don't.

In addition, you must offer value through various channels like social media, YouTube videos, or group chats. These are your opportunities to market yourself for free and show the public that you have a lot to offer. You don't have to put on full coaching sessions for free, but give your potential clients a taste of what you're about.

Solve Client Problems

The easiest and most effective way for a business coach to gain credibility is to help solve their client's problems as masterfully as possible. A client seeks out a business coach because they want strong guidance in creating a solid business. They want to overcome problems swiftly as they come upon them. This is what they want, so this is what you must give them. When you do, then they will know you are legitimate. When their friends and associates ask them how they were able to build up their business so well, they will tell them about you. Instantly, you just got a word-of-mouth shoutout. The more solutions you provide, the more credibility you will naturally gain.

Get Visible Immediately

If you want to make a name for yourself, whether it's with coaching or anything else, you must make yourself visible. You cannot hide in a bunker and expect people to know about you. Get out there on social media, YouTube, podcasts, and any other platform you can to get people to know about you. Nowadays, anyone can create podcasts or YouTube channels, so there's an extra benefit there. If you are willing to do speaking engagements, get out there and speak where you can. Be as visible as you can.

Be Trustworthy, Consistent, and Genuine

These three attributes are the cornerstone of credibility. People must know you are there to help them and not just in it for the money. Focus on improving these three principles and you will slowly build your credibility.

Be An Active Student and Contributor

Actively engage in the art of coaching with all of your heart and mind. Seek out professional training, read books, go to seminars, get a coaching mentor yourself, and do whatever you need to keep on learning. The more you are willing to improve your craft, the more credible you will become in the industry.

Hitch Your Wagon to Someone Else's Star

There are many coaching practices already out there with credibility and a strong reputation. Become a subcontractor with them and you will soon learn firsthand how to run a successful coaching business, the client and coaching process, marketing tips, and get a lot of firsthand experience. By being attached to an established brand, you will gain a lot of exposure in every aspect.

Many of the top coaches in the world have their own certification programs like John Maxwell or Tony Robbin. Getting certification through one of their programs can be greatly beneficial for you too.

Always Be Understanding

People have a desire to be understood. One of the major steps in gaining credibility is to demonstrate sincerity in understanding where your clients are at in their lives, their feelings, and what they are currently experiencing. After this, you must show your client that you can guide them to a proper solution that they may not be able to reach on their own. You are not telling them what to do, you are helping them find their own answers.

Volunteer in Visible Ways

Volunteering in your industry can be a great way to gain experience, connections, and credibility. Examples of places for volunteering in this manner include nonprofit organizations, colleges, and universities, or mission-driven organizations.

WHAT TO AVOID AS A COACH

Not only do you need to know how to gain credibility as a coach, but you must also know what to avoid doing. Mistakes can cost you a lot and put a complete halt to your coaching practice before it even has a chance to get off the ground. The following are some fatal errors you want to avoid at any point during your coaching process.

. . .

Fixing

Many people who like to help others become accustomed to stepping in and doing everything themselves. As a coach, this is something you want to avoid. Remember the example of the personal trainer from chapter one. Just like a trainer, a coach cannot fix their client's problems. they can simply guide them into finding their own answers. If you end up correcting all of your client's problems on your own, they will not know what to do when you're not around. Eventually, they will fall apart and will blame you for your poor coaching skills. Plus, you don't want to get the reputation of someone who simply fixes people's problems. Clients will just start taking advantage of you if this occurs.

Interrupting

As a coach, you are there to listen to your client and provide guidance. You are not there to interrupt and interject with your own points of view. Ask followup questions as appropriate, ask for clarification when needed, but don't interrupt. Wait until your client is done or a pause before you start speaking. Your client deserves to let all of their feelings out and will become frustrated if you constantly put up blockades that prevent them from speaking.

Distracted Coaching

Whether you are coaching online or in-person, avoid distracted coaching at all costs. This means limiting environmental noise.

Go to a peaceful cafe for a meeting rather than a loud restaurant. If possible, choose some type of office setting. When you are coaching, remain fully engaged. Don't try to multitask by doing other activities while trying to coach. Even if you are skilled at multitasking, you will either not be able to give your client the attention they deserve or won't appear to be giving that attention during a session and that is not fair to them.

Stacking Questions

The concept of stacking questions means that you are asking your client more than one question at a time. On the outset, this can cause mass confusion and make your client feel overwhelmed. Ask one question at a time and allow the client to answer fully before asking another question.

Checklist Coaching

Checklist coaching means that you are using a predetermined list of questions rather than targeted ones geared towards your client's needs. Remember that you want to look unique as a coach and checklist coaching means you are just following some status quo approach. Also, your client will have their personal set of issues they need to deal with, so using a cookie-cutter approach like checklist coaching will just make them feel like they are part of a crowd and not an individual person.

Being Diagnostic

This goes along the lines of telling your clients what to do. When you are being diagnosed, you are asking your client-specific questions and making targeted suggestions, like, "Have you tried this?" or "This is what you should do." This is the wrong path to take when coaching and more so falls within the lines of consulting. As a coach, you need to ask more open-ended questions without giving your clients definitive answers.

Getting Trained on the Client's Time

With each client, you will learn and improve your skills. That's a given. However, you cannot start taking clients until you can offer them something valuable. Therefore, before you start coaching on your own, get practice in other ways, like training with a partner, sitting in on coaching sessions, going through a qualified training program, or a combination of all of these. Do not get trained on the client's time.

Failing to Put in Ways to Track Progress

Coaching is about getting results for your client. You must also have a way to track these results so both parties can see the progress that's been made. Find your own unique ways to measure changes that have occurred.

Leading on a Client You Cannot Help

At some point, you may need to cut the cord with a client. You will not be the right coach for everybody. Once you realize that you don't have a connection for whatever reason, be honest with your client about it and refer them to a new coach. Do not lead them on if you don't think you can help them. A client will appreciate your honesty more than fake help.

All of these habits will put a bad taste in your client's mouth about you and the coaching profession, in general. You must avoid these habits at all costs. Once your reputation starts to suffer, it will be difficult to rebuild.

I hope you enjoyed these tips to help you increase your credibility as a business coach. The reputation of an entrepreneur means a lot for their success. Credibility leads to a positive reputation. Always remember that with anything you do with your coaching practice.

WHY VULNERABILITY IS IMPORTANT

Vulnerability

A common misconception throughout history is that the strongest people among us never show emotion, are always closed off, and avoid anything that makes them appear vulnerable. The truth is, vulnerability is extremely important for progress to be made. In the field of business coaching, we rely on our clients to become vulnerable insofar as they can communicate the extent of their problems, and as such help them the most. If a client remains closed off, there is no chance of reaching them. Since a vulnerable person does put their guard down and open themselves up emotionally, it is a true sign of strength. Here are some major reasons why vulnerability is so important and why you should start embracing it.

Vulnerability Allows Advancement

Making yourself vulnerable is a scary prospect. Trying anything new for the first time can be quite nerve-racking. It's okay to feel fear, but it's not okay to let this fear stop you from moving forward. You need to expand your comfort zone by taking some chances. When you take chances, you are making yourself vulnerable because you are entering unfamiliar territory where you don't know what is going to happen. In terms of a coaching session, this means opening up emotionally, allowing you to advance.

Vulnerability Leads to Increased Abilities

When you are guarding yourself, it means you are fearful of something, like getting harmed physically or emotionally, getting exposed, or a number of other things that threaten your safety. However, if you are willing to be vulnerable in a safe setting, you are getting past your fear of the unknown. A major fear that people have is that of failing. They hate the thought of failing at something and are worried about looking foolish. They have negative voices in their head telling them they can't do something. When they give in to these voices, they are refusing to be vulnerable.

Once you learn how to be vulnerable, you start taking risks. Remember that anytime you step out of your comfort zone, you are making yourself vulnerable. Even walking out of your home has an element of vulnerability to it. Once you start embracing this idea, you will accomplish more goals, challenge yourself more often, and increase your abilities, in general.

A client who becomes vulnerable is more likely to set out on specified action plans. This will lead to more desired results.

Vulnerability Allows Openness With Others

Once someone accepts their vulnerability, they become much more open about their lives. They will usually not hesitate to express any of their emotions. This can be a double-edged sword, depending on who a person's friends are. If they are close to other people who appreciate openness, it can be a good thing.

Having an openness to share is a huge blessing for any business coach. The more vulnerable a client is, the less exploration a coach will have to do in order to find answers. The more trust you establish with a client ahead of time, the more vulnerable they are willing to be.

Vulnerable Allows Openness to Self

Not only will vulnerability allow you to be more open with the public, but also more open and honest with yourself. Being vulnerable increases self-confidence because you are more willing to put yourself on the world's stage. You are inviting people to get to know you, both negative and positive aspects. By doing this, you are also opening yourself up for criticism which is truly brave. The more criticism you are willing to receive, the stronger you will grow.

As a coach, having a client who is open with themselves will also be more courageous in sharing during coaching sessions. They will also go out after a session and take chances which means they will follow through on their plans without becoming fearful.

Vulnerability Makes it Comfortable to be in Discomfort

Being vulnerable is all about leaving your comfort zone and becoming uncomfortable. As with anything else, the more often you put yourself in uncomfortable settings, the more you will get used to them. As a result, you will become more comfortable and willing to put yourself in vulnerable situations. The more you expose yourself to vulnerability, the greater potential for success you will have.

Other benefits of vulnerability include:

- Having more self-acceptance. Not being afraid of who you are, flaws, and all.
- Engaging in more real and truthful conversations.
- Attracting the right kind of people in your life.
- Being empathetic will be much easier.
- Strengthening the bond of many of your relationships.
- Appearing more humanized in other people's eyes. Most people don't like being around those who appear perfect all the time. They appreciate those who are willing to show some of their flaws.

Here's the bottom line, being vulnerable is scary, but it makes life more exciting and worth living. That old adage of nothing gets done inside of a comfort zone holds a lot of truth. To accomplish your goals and live the life you desire, you have to take chances which means you have to become vulnerable. As a coach, this is something you must also get across to your clients. Being a coach, it is important to have clients who are willing to be vulnerable, otherwise, you will get nowhere. In addition, if someone is planning to start a business, they will need to put themselves in positions of vulnerability often.

HELP YOUR CLIENT BECOME VULNERABLE

Since there are so many advantages to being vulnerable and being in this state will vastly improve the relationship between a coach and client, it is in your best interest as a coach to help your clients become more vulnerable. Ultimately, it is up to them how open they want to be, but here are a few ways you can guide them.

Help Them Accept That They Are Worthy

Before a person can become vulnerable, they must recognize that they are worthy of receiving a positive response from the world. Help them believe that who they are is enough to warrant love. Basically, a person needs to know and believe they are capable of reaching their goals.

As a coach, you can help your clients in this regard by reinforcing the fact that they are worthy. This is where asking great follow up questions comes in. When a client is able to reach their conclusion with the help of your guidance, they will start believing they can achieve what they want in life.

> *"...The people who have a strong sense of love and belonging believe they are worthy of love and belonging. That's it. They believe they are worthy."*
>
> — BRENE BROWN, VULNERABILITY RESEARCHER

Understand What a Person's Skittish Tendencies Are

Many people who are on the cusp of showing vulnerability will have a knee-jerk reaction at the last minute and retreat back to their familiar environment. That environment is one of being guarded. This reaction will seem appropriate in the moment, but most people will regret it once they feel they are in a safe place. Making the final jump when you are at that moment of truth is a better option that will make you happier in the end.

As a coach, there will be many moments where certain clients will be right there on the edge. They will want to open up but are not quite there yet. It will be very easy for them to retreat and without your intervention, they are more likely to do that. If you notice this hesitation or skittishness, you can guide and encourage your clients to keep moving towards vulnerability by using the skills of listening and asking appropriate questions. We will go over these skills later in this book.

One technique you can use with your client is to write down the emotions they feel when they are hesitant to be vulnerable. These emotions can be triggers and being aware of them can help in avoiding them in the future.

Help Clients understand They Can Deal With an Outcome

It is a horrible feeling when you put your emotions out there and get nothing back. However, once this happens, you feel the hurt, but that's as far as it goes. After feeling the pain and pulling yourself back up, you know that you can handle the aftermath of being vulnerable.

Help your clients understand this too. Have them discuss past moments of pain by putting themselves out there. Remind them that they are still here which means they survived. As a coach, you must also be a listening ear as they share their vulnerability. never dismiss or downplay their emotions because they are real to them.

Share Hurt With Others

Once again, you are in the perfect position as a coach to let your clients share their feelings and emotions. As your clients open up about their pain, whatever it may be, you have the opportunity to be a non-judgmental ear. As you are listening to your client, give them the time they need to fully express themselves before asking more questions. Never make them feel like they're being rushed. The more practice they get at being vulnerable, the better they will be at it.

Help Your Clients Realize They are on the Way Up

Avoiding vulnerability is actually counterproductive. People feel that they are protecting themselves when they remain closed off. However, they are just harming themselves more through inaction. Think about all of the benefits that come from vulnerability and now imagine that you are depriving yourself of all of them. This will continue to keep you in a state of disappointment.

Vulnerability does also have the potential to cause harm. That's always the case when you are taking a risk. However, if you try and fail, at least you will know. You can move on. If you remain closed off, you will stay at the bottom and never grow. If you are already at the bottom, the only way to go is up. As a coach, you can help your clients realize this through thoughtful questioning.

We spoke about credibility earlier. Credibility leads to trust, and trust leads to comfort. When your clients are comfortable around you, they are more likely to become vulnerable. Always work on building your credibility as a business coach.

THE IMPORTANCE OF PRIVACY

All of us at Elvin Coaches have worked with countless clients who have expressed their deepest concerns, desires, goals, fears, and feelings. Oftentimes, our clients will tell us things that their best friends and closest family members do not know. They put a lot of trust in us by doing this and we must all remember to take this trust very seriously.

This is why it is important to always maintain privacy when working with a client. Treat the information they give you like you would handle protected medical information. It is not appropriate to discuss what your clients tell you with other people. What happens in the session should stay in the session.

3

TIME MANAGEMENT TIPS TO INCREASE PRODUCTIVITY

"The key is not in spending time, but investing it."

— STEPHEN R. COVEY

Time management is such a critical subject that many books already cover. Time management is a skill that is highly necessary but woefully ignored by many segments of the population. This is a shame because so many goals and dreams get crushed because people do not use this essential resource well. As the above quote suggests, our time must be invested because it is the most valuable resource we have.

A subset of business coaching is time management coaching. Many coaches and managers alike, will immediately review a client or employee's general performance and immediately come to the conclusion that their time management skills are poor. Furthermore, as they view their existing options for increasing performance, they feel that none of them will be beneficial. The truth is, in order to make a lasting difference, coaches need to look outside the box beyond the limited options in front of them to create a much larger context for their clients to succeed.

(Chuangch, n.d.)

TIME MANAGEMENT COACH STRATEGIES

As we mentioned earlier, you can make time management a major part of your program as a business coach or become a time management coach exclusively. In this section, we will go over some options you have as a time management coach to help your clients in this regard.

Give Them a Bunch of Tips

With this approach, it is as simple as observing someone as they function through the day and randomly tossing them tips on how to manage their time. For example, you can randomly say, "A planner is a great way to keep your schedule organized," or "Have you tried a to-do list before?" This strategy is not the best because time management is based on the accumulation of a number of habits that are developed over time. You can't break these habits simply by telling someone to do something. Just like it takes a while to build, it will take a while to break and reform.

Changing habits means you must shift many ingrained patterns of behavior. Some people have held onto their habits since they were small children and learned from the influential adults in their lives. Before you attempt your first coaching session, it helps to know and understand what specific habits your client has. From here, you can systematically help them shift from their good to bad habits for improving time management.

Buy a Book

Buying someone a book can be a better option than tossing tips because it gives a client something concrete to look at to obtain some time management advice. The only problem here is that everyone gets their own interpretation from reading a book. This is not necessarily a bad thing, but coaches must realize their clients will not do things just as they do.

Also, from a book, you get a singular approach to handling a situation. We are all different from each other and that means a one-size-fits-all method may not be very effective. A customized approach is much more useful for coaching clients, and in reality, that is your job as a business coach. A book is an okay option, but you should also review it with them and see what they think. Therefore, make sure it is a book you have read and understand well.

Time Management Program

This can be a good option too and a client may get more personalized attention, but still not to the extent of working with a coach. Another major issue with time management programs is the lack of followup. Participants will leave feeling inspired but revert back to their old habits because they have taken no real action to make habit changes.

Effective Techniques for Time Management

The following are some general steps for creating good time management that you can help your clients achieve.

Scheduling

Creating a tangible schedule is essential for making sure you get everything you need to be done completed. You can use a scheduling app on your phone or a physical planner, whichever one you prefer. When making a schedule:

- Create a long-term plan, preferably about a month, or several months in advance.
- Assess that work that needs to be completed weekly and daily.
- Adjust the plan based on specific needs.

Create a Daily Checklist

- Spend five to ten minutes each day planning your activities using a to-do list.
- Review and prioritize your list before you get moving. Make sure you are doing the most important and complicated tasks first.
- Break down the complicated tasks into smaller and manageable steps.
- As you complete items, check them off your list. It's important to finish one task before moving onto the next one.

Create a Habit

- Establish a routine of completing these lists.
- Spend time each week reviewing your list and goals. This is to make sure you are keeping up and assessing for any changes in your plan.
- Reward yourself when sticking to your routines.
- Keep a calendar of your long-term schedule with you.

Balance Your Life

- Make every minute of your day count.
- Prioritize your tasks from the most important to least important.
- When you are focused on a task or activity, remain committed to it without distractions. When you are working, focus on working. When you are spending time with friends, remain fully engaged with them.
- Don't procrastinate.

Time

WHY PROCRASTINATION IS BAD

We certainly cannot talk about time management without discussing it's close relative, procrastination. Procrastination is a major productivity killer and probably the greatest culprit in creating poor time management. Procrastination basically means you are putting off something for later that can be done now. In most cases, this is an important task that has a deadline but is not very appealing to work on. As a result, people will substitute something less important or a time-wasting for the task they don't want to work on. As a result, they get closer to the deadline and will have less time to get it done. This will lead to more stress and anxiety which will also cause a reduction in performance.

When you procrastinate, you are not using your time well. Imagine having a project that is due at the end of the week. You can start it on Monday and put in a couple of hours each day so that on the final day, you will just have to touch a few things up. Instead, you don't work on it on Monday, Tuesday, or Wednesday, and then on Thursday, you realize the mistake you made. Not only do you have to work on the project from scratch, but you also have to make sure it is presentable. Procrastination can affect us in many ways and it is a habit we need to get rid of.

Procrastination is often confused with pure laziness. This is not the case. There are usually some more underlying issues going on like having a fear of failure, fear of success, being a perfectionist, or having some underlying emotional issues. Furthermore, extended procrastination can lead to more mood disorders down the line. The following are some steps you can help your clients with if they display signs of being a procrastinator.

Recognize Being a Procrastinator

If a person is delaying important tasks for a genuinely good reason, like something more urgent coming up or taking some time to think about a project before jumping in, then it's not actually procrastination. It is a purposeful delay. However, if they are putting things off indefinitely or for no apparent reason, then procrastination is the culprit. Some other signs of procrastination include:

- Filling up the day with low-priority tasks.
- Leaving items on a to-do list for long periods of time.
- Getting distracted constantly while working on something important.
- Doing unimportant tasks for other people.
- Not knowing how to say no.
- Waiting to be in the right mood to complete a task.

The first step in solving a problem is acknowledging that you have one. As a time management coach, help your client figure out if they are procrastinators.

. . .

Work Out the Reason for Procrastination

After figuring out someone is a procrastinator, the reasons behind the habit must be determined. As we stated earlier, it is generally not related to laziness and there are usually more underlying reasons. For example, are you procrastinating on something because you find it boring and tedious? The best thing to do in this situation is to get it out of the way as quickly as possible. This way, you can stop worrying about it and move on. Why keep something in the back of your mind that you don't want there?

Poor organization, fear, overconfidence, and perfectionism are all common reasons for procrastination. Work with your client to determine why they are procrastinators.

Adopt Some Anti-Procrastination Strategies

Procrastination is a deeply ingrained habit and if your client is like most people, many of those around them were probably the same way. Habits only stop controlling us when we actively stop doing them. Below are a few strategies to tell your client so they can kick the self-defeating habit of procrastination:

- Forgive yourself for procrastinating in the past. There is nothing you can do about past mistakes, so it's best to let them go and move on. This will give you a more positive view of yourself.
- Commit to a task and focus on doing instead of

avoiding. Specify a time for completing your tasks. A trick you can use is to make a personal deadline that is a couple of days earlier than the actual deadline.

- Promise yourself a reward if you complete a difficult task on time and an even bigger reward if you complete it a little early.
- Have someone hold you accountable. When we feel someone is watching us, we tend to be more careful with what we do.
- Take care of things as you go. People have a tendency to ignore items as they become aware of them. However, it is better to tackle them from the get-go as long as it's not interrupting an important task. For example, if you get some important emails, answer them right away. If an appliance breaks, take care of it ASAP. If you need to make some phone calls, get them over with. As you put off the small things, they will slowly build up into a large pile.
- Minimize distractions by turning off your social media, avoid answering emails, work in a quiet area, let people know not to bother you during certain hours, and don't keep anything on your desk that does not need to be there.

Many of the time management techniques we will address later will also help you with procrastination. Get rid of this evil cousin of time management and you will be surprised at the progress you make. Of course, procrastination is not the sole reason for poor time management, so you may need to dig a little deeper to figure out.

HOW TO BUILD A HABIT

Proper time management has a lot to do with the habits you develop. Habits are the tendencies you develop over time and directly affect what you do during the day and how well you perform. Even procrastination is a habit that is built throughout the years, and it must be broken down and replaced with a new habit. Since habits are essential to success, we will go over some steps on creating new habits that you can help your client with.

Focus On One Habit at a Time

There is a term known as ego depletion which refers to a person's diminished capacity to regulate their emotions and actions. This phenomenon impedes our ability to form new habits because our willpower supply is spread out among all areas of our lives and there is only so much to go around. Therefore, trying to work on changing or creating multiple habits at once can seem impossible. This is why it's important to focus on one habit at a time. By doing this, your willpower will be channeled into focusing on one area, which will be more effective in the long run.

To increase the odds of success, choose one habit you want to focus on and learn everything you can do to it right. Since the focus of this book is business, we can help our clients determine what tendency is negatively impacting their business the most and work on correcting that. For example, if they are waking up late and don't have enough time to prepare for the day, we can help them work on changing this habit.

If your client thinks they have the willpower to change more than one habit at a time, they can certainly try. However, don't have them push it too much.

Commit to a Minimum of Thirty Days

There has been a lot of discussion on the amount of time it takes to officially turn a practice or routine. For example, how long will a person have to wake up by a certain time before it becomes natural? While the time frame can vary with every individual, a major consensus seems to be at least twenty-one days. This means you must perform a routine for twenty-one days straight before it can officially become a habit (Scott, 2016).

For this section, we will be extra cautious and give thirty days. When you are working with your client on developing their new habit, give them a timeframe of at least thirty days. At this point, you can assess and determine if more time is needed. Don't be too hung up on the length of time because the client should be allowed to move at their own pace. The timeline is just something to use as a reference.

. . .

Anchor the New Habit to an Established Habit

A new habit will be much easier to incorporate into a routine if it gets tied to an existing habit. For example, if you generally exercise every day, you can tell yourself that you will wake up earlier in the mornings to have more time for exercise. The following are some other examples:

- After I come home and change out of my work clothes, I will immediately change into my workout clothes and go for a run.
- After I get my kids ready for school, I will immediately plan my day ahead.

Anchor your habit to something you already do and it will become much easier to transition.

Take Baby Steps

You are not going to change overnight. There are very few instances of that actually happening. The only way to make a habit stick is by making it an automatic behavior that you perform naturally. You can get to this point by taking baby steps to create a new level of commitment. The objective is to create micro-commitments where it's nearly impossible to fail. If you want to wake up an hour earlier in the morning, start by making small milestones:

- Get up five minutes early on the first day with the goal of making it to twenty minutes by the end of the first week.
- Make a goal of reaching forty minutes by the end of week two.
- Your final goal will be to make sixty minutes by the end of week three.

These steps are simple, but they will require commitment. Keep doing them without missing a day.

Make a Plan for Obstacles

While you are creating a new habit or going after a goal, there will be plenty of obstacles along the way. While you cannot see all of them coming, you must prepare the best you can for most of them. Foresee potential obstacles that will come your way and do your best to plan for them. Examples of these include:

- Time
- Weather
- Other people
- Space
- Self-consciousness

Always anticipate obstacles and never assume it will be smooth sailing. Otherwise, you will be caught off guard constantly and this will be a major time-waster.

Create Accountability for Your Habit

When you create accountability for what you say, you are more likely to follow through on it. The great thing here is that your client will already have an accountability partner, and that is you as their coach. If a client knows you will be following up with them about what they've done as far as their habits, they are more likely to keep their goals.

You can also have your client find accountability partners in their personal lives, like friends or family members, to help them when you are not there.

Reward Important Milestones

Building a habit will take a lot of effort along the way. You will have a long road ahead and you should not wait until the end to reward yourself. You can give yourself rewards for smaller milestones along the way. This will help you to keep moving forward.

TIME IN TERMS OF PHILOSOPHY

We want to spend this section discussing the philosophy behind time and what it means to so many people. Many individuals in the modern world see time as money and if they are wasting it, they are essentially losing money. This can spill over into regretting time with family and friends or doing the thighs they love. During these moments, people who view time as money become angry, frustrated, or anxious because they are doing something that's not making them financially richer.

Unfortunately, when people live with this mindset, they are putting less value on their time because they are making a finite value out of it. Instead, people should see their time as priceless, since they have a limited amount of it that will never come back. Each second that passes, is a second that's gone for good. This is why it's so important to invest our time into a life that we get pleasure from. Yes, we need to work, and many of us want to accomplish great things while we are around. However, it is essential to use our minutes towards living a life we enjoy.

If people only look at time as a chance to make money, then anything they do outside of that realm will be a waste to them, and therefore, will never enjoy their present moment. Think of this example for a moment. You are sitting at a table with a good friend. You are there simply to relax and have a good conversation. However, your mind is preoccupied with the money you are not making while sitting at this table instead of working. As a result, you have wasted this precious time to talk to your friend. You can place yourself in any other situation and get similar feelings. How often do we hear stories about busy professionals who are too busy to spend time with their kids, spouses, or friends? These individuals are not too busy, they are just prioritizing work and money over valuable relationships.

From now on, ask yourself if you are using your time wisely. Are you enjoying it, investing it, and living the best life you can?

Are you simply focused on financial gain? If you thought about time as a finite resource that will soon be gone, would you use it differently? Think about this and determine where you want to go from here.

MANAGE YOUR TIME

Now that we have established the importance of time management, we will go over some essential time management techniques. In reality, we do not manage time because time keeps moving. We have no ability to stop it or slow it down. Plus, everybody has the same number of hours in a day. We are actually managing ourselves and what we are focusing our minds, actions, and energy towards.

The best time management techniques change the way we work, get rid of distractions, improve our concentration, and increase our overall productivity. There are numerous strategies floating around out there, but these are the ones we feel make the biggest difference.

Be Intentional By Keeping a To-Do List

While a to-do list is not a groundbreaking technique, it has been overlooked by many as an effective time management tool. Simply writing things down that need to get done can help ensure important tasks are not missed and we also save time trying to remember things. To-do lists can be broken down into different categories based on the type of tasks that need to be completed.

Having a list of tasks keeps you intentional on what you need to work on. By creating one, you are effectively laying out in words what needs to be completed. Never underestimate the power of writing things down. When your mind does wander, refer back to your list to keep yourself on track. As you complete items on your list, scratch them off so you don't have to wonder about them anymore.

There are many to-do list apps you can download. Also, you can use the old school pen-and-paper method. Whatever you don't get done on your list in one day, move over to the next. Just make sure the items you move are the less critical ones.

To-Do List

Prioritize Your Tasks

After writing out your to-do list, rank your tasks from highest priority to least priority and, of course, perform the higher priority tasks first. Doing this guides you through the activities of the day and ensures that the most critical tasks are taken care of. Prioritize what is important to you and not other people when making out your list.

Without prioritization, we often focus our attention on the wrong things in life. In addition, our attention goes towards pressing tasks that have a deadline, but we forget out the important projects too. Determine the tasks that will have the most positive effect on you, your work, and your team.

Manage Distractions

Distractions can come out of nowhere and get the best of all of us at some point. No matter how hard we try, distractions are unavoidable to a certain degree. We can be working hard and then decide to check emails or our social media accounts. Before we know it, more time has passed and we effectively became victims of a major distraction. Not only do we have to contend with the distraction itself, but also the time it takes to refocus on our original task, which can also be several minutes.

Distractions can come from many different sources and it's important to identify and eliminate them as much as possible during our working hours. Some common culprits include the aforementioned email and social media, television, background noise, phones and tablets, people, or anything in our environment that should not be there.

Timely is a great app for identifying and quantifying distractions. It can automatically record the time you spend on every work tool and website to see where all of your time is going. Apps like StayFocused or Mindful Browsing can put access restrictions on time-wasting websites. Also, log out of your emails, social media accounts, and other applications when you are not working on them. Disable popups or notifications. Keep your desk clear from anything that is not work-related. This includes snacks. If you get hungry, physically get up and eat. If snacks are close by, then you will be distracted much more often by taking small bites.

Distractions

Block Times For Your Work

Often, people work in small spurts between trying to take care of other activities like grocery shopping, picking up their kids, cooking dinner, or doing the laundry. However, to be the most effective with your time, you must block out certain portions of your schedule that will solely be dedicated to working. Time blocking protects your workspace and puts some healthy pressure on you to complete it.

Instead of juggling between many jobs, thinking you will get more done this way, focus on one job at a time. You will actually be more productive this way. There is a major myth out there about multitasking. People believe this is the only way to get everything done when in reality, less work is getting done and the outcomes are worse. This is because it is impossible to work on multiple things at the same time and still give each of them the same amount of focus.

Set aside time for administrative tasks too, like sending emails, filing, or making phone calls. These activities should not be part of your main workload.

Be Self-Aware and Track Your Time

Before you can start improving how you use your time, you need to understand how you use it in the first place. Tracking your time provides insights and self-awareness to make effective changes. When you perform this strategy, you become more aware of hidden items that drain your time and inefficient processes.

Fortunately, there are apps you can use to track your time to avoid having to do it manually. They will record your time and put it in a private timeline while you go about your day.

Employ some of these time management strategies with your clients to see how they work for them.

WHO ARE YOUR PROSPECTIVE CLIENTS?

A time management coach is along the same lines as a productivity coach. These types of coaches are essential in the business world because of the competitive nature and the need to get more work done in less time and with equal or greater results. Improving productivity will save companies a lot of time and money. Also, they will be putting out superior products and services in minimal amounts of time.

If you have the desire to become a productivity coach, you will be in high demand because you will be needed to guide organizations to achieve higher outputs without putting in the extra effort.

A good productivity coach is someone who can thoroughly guide their clients to work smart. By using the right tools, plus some logical and practical approaches to every activity, the coach can help their clients maximize results. As a coach in this sector, you will be able to observe your client's performance. You will be able to view their strengths and weaknesses. Finally, you will be able to help them simplify their daily routines, so they don't feel overwhelmed. If you are interested in all of this, then this line of coaching may be right up your alley. The following list summarizes what your role will entail.

- Supporting the client with a plan based on their goals.
- Helping define the objectives of a goal.

- Assisting clients in maintaining a work-life balance.
- Guiding clients on increasing sales and profits.

You will have plenty of business too once people become aware of your work. Many individuals in the business world become stressed and frustrated with all that they have going on and this severely affects their productivity and output. When you come in, you can help them develop better skills to improve their confidence, performance, and productivity. We will go over some of the prospective clients that you will have as a business coach.

Entrepreneurs

Entrepreneurs spend a lot of time on many different aspects of their business and mighty be doing everything themselves, especially if they are new. With all of the different responsibilities and distractions, they are bound to lose focus on their work which will severely reduce their output. A productivity coach will help them manage their time better. They can help entrepreneurs streamline their work, gain more clarity, and ultimately, increase their productivity.

Entrepreneurs are looking for ways to obtain better returns on investments. The tools provided by a productivity coach can help them implement the correct plans and strategies for higher profits. As a productivity coach, you will be very valuable to an entrepreneur.

Multinational Companies

Employees who work for multinational companies are always under a lot of pressure to show productivity. For their superiors, this is a measure of their worth to the company. Multinational companies need to get results, or they will cease to exist. For this to occur, they need a well-thought-out plan and a business coach is a perfect person to help them develop one.

A business coach can help these organizations by supporting them in finding solutions and achieving better sales results. Finally, a coach can provide the necessary tools that can develop various skills for a company's employees. This will help them with time management and effectively increase their productivity.

Educational Institutions

Educational institutions are always looking for ways to improve the productivity of their teaching staff and student body. These institutions want positive results from their students because it is a reflection on them too, and they also want to assess the effectiveness of their teaching methods. After analyzing the methods, coaches can train teaching staff in new skills and methods that will lead to students achieving better results on their exams and projects.

Time management and productivity are some of the most crucial skills to develop for success in the business world. You will help individuals greatly by focusing your efforts in these areas.

STEPS TO INCREASE PRODUCTIVITY

As a productivity coach, you can use certain steps to help improve your client's productivity. While you cannot tell your client what to do, you can certainly suggest some tips on how to increase productivity and overall performance. These traits will determine how much they actually get done toward setting up their business and other work. We will go over some simple strategies for productivity right here.

Schedule your work

Your clients can get into the habit of planning their work ahead of time. this means they should set aside 10-15 minutes every morning, or before they go to bed to plan out what their day will be like. This will eliminate the time wasted on wondering what needs to get done. Write it all done, prioritize, and follow the list you make.

Use Your Most Productive Hours Wisely

Many self-help gurus and even life coaches out there push the idea of waking up earlier to get more done. This strategy can work for some people, especially those who are early birds. However, the key to productivity is to use the hours in the day where you are most energetic and do as much of your important work as you can during these times. So, if you have more energy in the morning, wake up early and get your important work done then. If you are a night owl, then stay up late working and completing important tasks. If you get energy in the afternoon, take advantage of these hours.

Help your client figure out what hours of the day they work best in. Encourage them to take advantage of these productive hours by doing as much as they can.

Organize Life on a Weekly Basis

Plan out your week on Sunday night. You don't have to have everything written down since you will still be making daily lists, but you should have a general idea of what your week will look like. In doing this, the client will have a sense of what steps they will take when on their most vital projects.

Treat All Days as Special

Every day of the week should be treated as special, even if it's a day meant for relaxation. Use the following list as an example:

- Sunday: Plan the week ahead.
- Monday: Work on Budgeting.
- Tuesday: Update marketing plan.
- Wednesday: Plan for any meetings or conferences.
- Thursday: Order inventory.
- Friday: Stock inventory.
- Saturday: Relaxation day.

Have a Review at the End of Each Day

When your day is all said and done, sit down and review what you were able to do and if you met all of your goals. If not, see where you need to make some changes.

Productivity is an essential part of running a business and a productivity coach can be essential in making a difference for the client.

4

MARKETING COACHING

Starting and building up a business is tedious work that often seems never-ending. There are many unanswered questions and several uncertainties on the horizon. Starting a business is a big risk and you have the potential to create something big or fail badly. Up to this point, we have discussed the benefits of having a business coach to help us develop a business plan from start to finish and manage our time properly. Another major aspect of running a business is marketing. Without a good marketing plan, your business will be lucky to get off the ground because no one will know that it exists.

Marketing is very tricky, especially with the advent of so many platforms and various techniques to get your post shown on various websites. As a business owner, many try their hand at this process without having to understand what SEO content means or what click funnels are. Marketing has become a science and the days of putting an ad in the local paper are a thing of the past.

Since marketing is quite complicated yet very important for a business, a marketing coach can be an essential partner in getting your business' name out there.

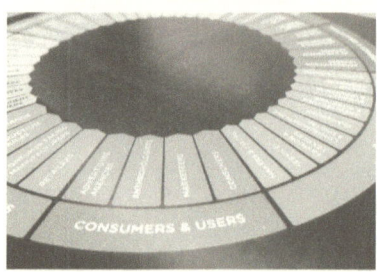

Marketing

WHO IS A MARKETING COACH?

A marketing coach is someone who works with business owners and managers to develop strategies with the goal being an increase in revenue without the business owner putting in extra time for marketing. Whether a business wants to increase its online sales or reach a broader segment of the market, a marketing coach will have the knowledge and skills to create an action plan for both.

Since proper marketing is vital to the success of a business, the skills of a marketing catch can be invaluable. What are some of the specific ways a coach can help in this sector? The following are a few examples:

- Helping the business owner stay focused on the remainder of the important business processes.
- Eliminating many of the errors during the marketing process so that less effort, money, and time get wasted.
- Implementing efficient and effective marketing strategies to obtain superior outcomes quickly.
- Helping avoid the shiny objects, or "magic bullets" that will supposedly revolutionize the way marketing is done. There are many scams out there that promise the world when you engage in certain marketing strategies. A good marketing coach can be there to identify these scams and sift them out.
- Developing long-term plans for marketing that will continuously help the business grow.

A good marketing coach can also guide a business owner at when, why, and how a specific marketing tool should be used. For example, they can decide to:

- Redesign a website
- Start a business blog
- Go on a podcast or start a podcast
- Engage in social media or LinkedIn marketing

With a marketing coach by your side, you will have less anxiety when trying to find ways to promote your business.

· · ·

Characteristics of a Marketing Coach

While marketing coaches can come from all different backgrounds and have specific skill sets, there are three essential characteristics that all marketing coaches must possess. These traits are the foundation of how they approach their client's needs.

- Empathy for the clients. This means there is an emotional connection and the coach is able to feel what their clients are going through. This is almost like walking in a person's shoes.
- An unwavering curiosity to hone their marketing skills. Marketing trends are continuously changing and a good coach will always keep up on the trends, tools, and ideas that are bringing in the best results.
- The ability to influence their clients through effective communication, management, and leadership skills.

A Good Marketing Plan

Just like any other business, a coach should not spend a dime on marketing until they have a solid plan to figure out what they are doing. Otherwise, you are just throwing your money at the wall and seeing if it sticks. As a business owner, you must value money because it can be hard to come by in many instances. Many coaches out there start up their practice without having any idea how they will generate leads or attract new clients. Therefore, they will not gain any business or make profits.

Create a solid marketing plan to help your business flourish. Your marketing plan must clearly state who you will be targeting with your services. For example, are you going to be a general business coach or get more specific into the subsets like a productivity or time management coach? Do you plan to work with a particular age group, as adults in their twenties, a certain gender, or people with specific socioeconomic backgrounds? Your marketing plan must also identify how you plan on finding clients and what you will need to do to make all of this happen.

Businesses generally fail because they don't have a steady stream of customers. This is because they fail to plan in so many ways, including their marketing. If you have a unique understanding of marketing or like to help a specific type of business, becoming a marketing coach can be a great option for you. You will have many potential clients including:

- Small business owners
- Managing directors/CEOs
- Small to medium enterprises (SMEs)
- Large organizations
- Marketing teams
- Entrepreneurs of all kinds

WHY DO BUSINESSES HIRE A MARKETING COACH?

A marketing coach can be a great investment for any type of business, whether large or small. No matter what sector or industry you are in, potential customers and clients must know that you exist. Proper marketing is essential for this to occur. Therefore, a great marketing coach can be worth their weight in gold. As a marketing coach yourself, you will be highly valuable to all types of business owners.

Small Businesses

A business that is in the initiation phases may not have the budget or finances available to test out various marketing strategies. The last thing you want to do as a new business owner is to throw money away on things that don't work. What will work is finding a high-quality coach who can guide you in the right direction. A good marketing coach will combine the ideas and passions of the business owner with their own unique marketing strategies to build an effective action plan for success.

Many techniques, tools, and programs, will help boost growth for your small business. The following are some special ways that a marketing coach can help:

- The coach will guide them in not short-selling themselves. Business owners have the right to charge what their product or service is worth, so don't sell

yourself short in this regard. A good coach can help you determine what you're selling is worth so they don't underprice themselves.
- The coach will help a business find their ideal clients. This will definitely help you generate some leads.
- The coach will also guide a business owner on how to be prepared when their business starts to ramp up. The coach will make sure the owner is not overwhelmed and continue to remain afloat.

New small business owners are naive to many things and no matter how many books you read or seminars you attend, you will be bombarded with many different issues. These will be enough to bring anyone down, and that is why so many business owners fail. A marketing coach can help you keep your business running strong. They will have your back through good and bad times.

Big Businesses

Some businesses have been around for many years and their situation is much different than a new business owner. For experienced business owners, the entrepreneurial spark is often gone or diminished. They get bored and let their guard down. What they need in times like these are new marketing strategies that will make their businesses thrive again. Many of these owners have not kept up with the latest marketing platforms and are still stuck in the old school methods.

A marketing coach can help such businesses and their owners remain on par with their competition by staying up to date on new marketing techniques. The coach will guide the business owners on how to leverage current marketing platforms which can be very complicated.

Any size business can benefit from the wisdom, connections, and experience of a marketing coach. The following are some of the sectors a coach should have a command of that a business owner can look for:

- Management
- Creating operational systems
- Marketing and Finance
- Developing sales
- Merchandising for retail
- Training employees

Of course, the main reason for hiring a coach is to help create a marketing plan that will succeed. No matter what kind of business it is, like an online, physical store, food, clothing, industrial, or anything else, you need to craft a winning marketing message and an ultimate client profile.

A marketing message will be the first thing your client's main audience will notice. You need to make a good first impression. To make a great client profile, focus on industries where you feel the most comfortable. For example, if you are more familiar with the retail and food industry, you should stick to these areas at first and avoid corporate businesses. Do this at least at the very beginning until you gain more experience. As a coach, to make a marketing plan work, you must focus on the following:

- Get in-depth knowledge of the actual business for which the marketing plan needs to be built around. Understand everything you can about the business, including all goals and needs.
- Don't try to experiment with all of the marketing strategies out there. Instead, trust the platforms and ways that you think will bring the most return on investment. For instance, LinkedIn marketing might be more effective for corporate businesses than Facebook or Instagram marketing, whereas Instagram might be the best for creative pathways, like art, painting, or photography.
- Always take your client's budget into account. You do not want to run them dry trying to market their business. Assess what your client has and what they are willing to spend on marketing. Do not create your plan until you analyze the financial position of your client. For a startup business, you may need to focus on more organic marketing techniques, rather than paid. Bigger businesses with larger budgets will likely go for paid marketing strategies.
- Create short-term marketing plans and move on. Your

marketing efforts will need time to build up and won't show results all at once. Always include small, actionable steps in your plan and have SMART goals.

SPECIFIC MARKETING STRATEGIES

For the final section of this chapter, we will describe some common marketing strategies to give you an idea of what direction you can take.

Building a Website

With everything being on the internet these days, it is hard to imagine a business not having a website or some type of online presence. A good website that is eye-catching is the most important ingredient for efficient marketing. It makes it possible for people all over the world to find you. As a marketing coach, you must be aware of how to drive traffic back to a website using innovative techniques. This includes designing websites that attract clients, click funnels, and SEO content. You must have a thorough knowledge of content marketing basics and how to generate leads for your client through their website.

Even the smallest businesses out there have websites or a web presence through social media. It's hard to run a business of any kind without one, so if your client is not at this level yet, it could be a recommendation that needs to be made.

Website Marketing

Promo-Kit

A promo-kit is also a great marketing technique to get people to view your work. It might seem obsolete to a certain degree since everything can be found online, but a good promo-kit can still hold some value. The following are some items to keep together for this tool:

- Audiotaped and videos
- Articles
- Media quotes or mentions
- Brochures
- Resumes
- Headshots

Classified Ads

Classified ads are low-cost and a great way to market yourself on a regular basis. You can use these types of ads to offer free sessions, products, articles, and other items related to your client's business.

Newsletters

Newsletters have become an old school method of marketing, but they are still very relevant today. A newsletter can be used to pass along a lot of valuable information about a business and the products or services they provide. As a marketing coach, it is important to learn how you can utilize newsletters for the benefit of your client's business.

Referrals

A marketing coach can guide their clients on how to increase their referral flow. This is similar to word-of-mouth marketing which is still one of the most effective methods. People who had a good experience with you telling other people are still marketing gold. Building a channel of new clients from existing ones demands much effort. With smart strategies, this can attract many clients. To get a proper referral flow, you must find a good balance between being too pushy and being too passive.

Press Releases

Press releases can greatly enhance the media presence of a business owner. As a marketing coach, this will be a big boost for your client. Press releases take a certain amount of skill and they can lead to more print media, radio or podcast interviews, and the chance to be shown on television.

. . .

Free Offerings

You might be wondering why free offerings should be given as you are trying to make money. However, this is a great marketing technique that tells your client you believe in your product or service. For example, you can give away free samples, or offer webinars and event workshops.

These various marketing strategies will work best based on what your goals are and what particular business you belong to. As a marketing coach, you can determine what techniques work best for your clients.

COMPLEMENTING WITH A BLOG

To help complement their coaching business, many individuals set up a blog where they write articles full of useful information. Potential clients find blogs very attractive because of how informative they are. A blog can be a small section of a website or a web page all on its own. Not only is blogging a great educational tool, but can help market too. Furthermore, once you learn how to set up a good blog, you can help your clients create one for their own businesses too.

A blog has to do three things:

- Acquire leads: These are from your readers who have an interest in your product or service.

- Nurture sales: Makes your prospects more likely to visit your sales page.
- Retain your customers: Helps to build up brand loyalty. When your clients feel like you add value to their lives, they tend to stay with you for the long haul.

The following are some of the key reasons why you should start a business blog:

- Drive more traffic to your website. Business blogging allows you to create great resources in the form of articles or posts that your prospective clients are looking for. These resources can include:
- Guides that completely cover a topic from start to finish.
- "How-to" articles that describe how to overcome some sort of challenge. For example, as a business coach, you can write a short "how-to" article on time management.
- A checklist with action steps to complete a task.
- Improve the search ranking for your website. When your prospects are searching online, they will be typing in some keywords. When you blog, you are bound to use some keywords related to your industry. The more often you blog, the higher the chances of your keywords and content being discovered.
- Build more readership and stronger relationships with

your customers. When people see you active online, they are more likely to engage with you. They will get to know you on a more intimate level too, which will help you sell your products or services. Blogging will provide a great connection between you and your customers, which will foster loyalty.
- Establish you and your brand as an industry leader. This relates to gaining credibility. If you regularly put out helpful and engaging content, clients will see you as more knowledgeable.
- It is very inexpensive to start and easy to set up. All you really need is a hosting website like WordPress or Weebly, which is very cheap. These hosting sites are also user friendly.
- Spur interactions with other industry leaders and prospective clients, especially when they start commenting on your posts. These types of engagements allow you to:
- Address any questions or concerns that prospects might have.
- Gain new topic ideas to research and write about.
- Get to know other bloggers and industry leaders.
- Helps nurture prospects towards an easier sale. The more content clients read about a product or service, the more likely they are to purchase it. Therefore, the more quality blogs you write, the easier it will be to make sales.

As your blog gets bigger, you can add followers, subscribers, and even people who want to pay for advertising on your site. It can become a side business on its own. With a blog, it's important to get it known, as well, by sharing it through multiple platforms. Other options that work in a similar fashion can be YouTube videos, podcasts, or social media groups. A blog is still easier to set up than YouTube or podcasts because certain equipment is needed, but these other choices have gotten simpler too.

There are many marketing options out there, so help clients find the best ones for them.

5

COMMON BUSINESS COACHING QUESTIONS

One of the most important items a coach will have in their arsenal is their ability to ask effective questions. This does not just mean asking the right questions, but also when to ask them and what tone to use. In many cases, it is not what you say, it is how you say it.

A conversation between a coach and a client rarely follows a perfect sequential path. However, by using the GROW model, a business coach can set up a nice framework to help structure their coaching sessions. Several managers of big companies have used the GROW Model with their employees as well. GROW stands for:

- Goal
- Reality (Current Reality)
- Options

- Will

It can be used by coaches and managers alike to improve performance, solve problems, make better and more informed decisions, learn new skills, and reach desired career goals.

The key to using the GROW models is to ask exceptional questions. The objective is not to tell people what to do, but to ask what is best for them. As a coach, it is your job to help clients come up with answers on their own through strategic questioning methods. think of yourself as a private investigator who is asking many followup questions until everyone has arrived at an answer. The GROW model is also a great way for new coaches to get used to asking appropriate questions. With experience, it will eventually become natural and automatic.

Questions=Answers

DISSECTING THE GROW MODEL

We will get more in-depth with the GROW Model and provide greater detail into what each step means. Within each step are specific questions you can ask the client.

Goal

Establishing a goal is the first step in the coaching process. This will lay the foundation for where the business coach and client will go. Goals can be categorized as performance goals, development goals, a problem that needs to be solved, important decisions to be made, or a goal just for a specific coaching session. Whenever you are discussing a goal with your clients, encourage them to make SMART goals, which stands for:

- Specific
- Measurable
- Attainable
- Realistic
- Timely

If a goal covers all of these factors, then it will be concrete and real. If you want to obtain financing for a business, a good goal statement can be: "I will be visiting at least five financial institutions this week to determine which one will give the best deal on interest rates and I plan to open a business loan by Friday that will cover my initial business expenses." This is a better statement than: "I want a million dollar loan to open a business." There is nothing really concrete about the second statement.

To help people gain clarity about their goals and make sure you're both on the same page, use the following questions:

- That specific goal do you want to achieve during this coaching session?
- What do you REALLY want right now?
- What overall goal do you want to achieve?
- What do you want to accomplish?
- What results do you want to accomplish?
- What is your ideal end result?
- What do you want to change the most?
- Why are you hoping to obtain this goal?
- What benefits would you obtain from accomplishing this goal?

Current Reality

This step in the GROW Method is to realize what your current situation is. Determine what is happening in your life, why it is happening, the context in which it is taking place, and the magnitude of the whole situation. During this step, the client needs to have time to think and reflect so they get the full scope of what is happening. The coach must display patience and allow their client the opportunity to really think everything through. This does not have to be a rapid-fire interrogation process.

Instead, ask appropriate questions and then sit back and wait for the response. Do not share your opinion or offer solutions. Just pay attention to your active listening skills. Get a clear understanding of your client's current reality with the following questions:

- What is happening to you now? What is the effect it is having?
- What steps have you taken towards your goal already if any?
- What is the best way to describe what you did?
- Where are you now in relation to where you want to be? How much further do you need to go?
- Where do you find yourself on a scale from 1-10?
- Regarding the success you have had so far, what do you feel is the largest contributor?
- What progress have you made thus far?
- What are you doing right now that is working well for you?
- What is required of you to reach your outcomes?
- What has stopped you from reaching your goal already?
- Do you know that other people have achieved similar goals to you?
- What have you already tried doing?

- What could you do better this time than in the past?
- On a scale of 1-10, how urgent is this situation?
- If you asked your friends what they think, what would they say about you?

Options

The third leg of the GROW Method is options. During this process, we help the client determine what they can do to reach their goals. The following questions will help your clients explore their options and generate solutions:

- What are all of your options?
- What do you believe you need to do next?
- What is a possible first step?
- What action do you think you need to take to achieve better results and get closer to your goal?
- What else could you do right now?
- Who else can help you with your goals?
- If you decided to do nothing, what would happen?
- What has already worked for you in your life? How can you do more of what worked?
- If you did more of what worked, what would happen?
- What is the most challenging part of that for you?
- What advice would you give to a friend about that?
- What would you gain or lose by saying or doing that?
- If someone did or said that to you what do you think would happen.

- What is the best/worst thing about this option?
- Which option out there are you ready to act on now?
- When you were in a similar situation before, how did you handle it?
- What things can you do differently now?
- Who out there has encountered a similar situation that you know of?
- If anything in the world was possible, and money or failure was not a factor, what would you do?
- What other options can you think of?

Will

This is the final portion of the GROW Method. The coach's job is to check for commitment and guide their clients in establishing a clear action plan. The following are some questions to help you search for and achieve commitments:

- How are you going to go about your goal?
- What actions do you need to take right now?
- How are you going to do that?
- How will you know when you have done it?
- What else can you do?
- What is the chance of your plan succeeding on a scale of 1-10?
- What is blocking your success right now?
- What other roadblocks are expected along the way?
- What resources exist that can help you?

- What is missing?
- What one small step can you take at this time?
- At what point are you going to start?
- When you reach success, what will that look like for you?
- What support systems do you need to reach this success you are imagining?
- What will happen if you don't take these actions?
- What do you need from others, including me, to help you achieve this?
- What are three sensible actions you can take this week towards your success?
- On a scale of 1-10, how committed are you to do what you say?
- What would it take to make your scale reach 10?

The GROW Method is a great way to get inside your client's mind and find out what they really want in their lives. the best part is, you don't have to tell them as they will slowly come to a realization on their own. If you noticed, there were very few, if any, "yes" or "no" questions. These are something you want to avoid because they can close off a conversation right away. Instead, focus on open-ended questions which will lead to follow-up questions based on your client's answers.

Growth

Business Focused Questions

To round out this chapter, we will go over some business-related questions using the GROW Method. As a business coach, you can ask your clients these questions to help them, and their businesses, grow. Once again, these questions are a great way to start a coaching and client session:

- What do you want your business to be known for? If someone were to write an article or film about it, what would they write?
- At its peak, what is your business like?
- What is the most important thing personally about what you do?
- What specific things does your business do really well?
- What is dissatisfying to you at the moment?
- If you could go back to the beginning of the year, or at least several months, what business advice would you give yourself?

- When your customers or competitors look at your business, what do they see?
- When you look at the progress of your business up to this point, on a scale of 1-10, how satisfied are you?
- If your satisfaction rating is not at a ten, what do you need to get it there?
- Looking forward to the next Christmas, imagine yourself being extremely excited by all of your accomplishments. As you look back, what would you have achieved to create this excitement?
- Over the next six months, what are three words that sum up your ideal self-image as a business owner?

Remember that your skills at asking questions can make or break a coaching session.

QUESTIONING TECHNIQUES

"The answers you get depend on the questions you ask."

— THOMAS KUHN

The above quote is definitely astute because if you want certain types of answers, you must ask certain types of questions. The questions you ask will not only lead to the information you get but also the relationships you develop. It will also help you avoid misleading people which is very important for you as a business coach.

In this section, we will review some of the everyday types of questions people ask and the responses they are likely to elicit.

Closed Questions

These are the types of questions we generally avoid during a coaching session. They generally invite one-word answers and limit following up questions. Of course, you can also swerve back around and keep questioning your clients, even after asking closed questions. If it only requires a "yes" or "no answer, it is considered a closed question. These are great for breaking the ice. For example, you can ask someone you just met if they are doing okay today. Also, if you want a quick answer, these questions will be useful at that time, as well. Once again, these will rarely be used in a coaching session where a relationship needs to be developed.

Open Questions

Open-ended questions require a lot more thought and are generally followed by a longer response. Some examples would be:

- Where do you see yourself in ten years?
- What are the best options you see for yourself moving forward?

These types of questions leave room for proper follow-up and keep the conversation moving forward. These are the perfect types of questions for a coaching session.

Probing Questions

These questions are great for gaining some clarification about what was said and encourages others to share more information. Probing questions usually come in a series that digs deeper into a situation and provide a larger picture of what is going on. For example, you can ask someone, "How soon do you want to get started, what topics do you want to discuss, and how long do you want our meeting to be?" Based on the responses, you can ask further probing questions. Probing questions are great to help avoid misunderstandings and gain more information from people who are reluctant.

Leading Questions

Leading questions are designed to lead an individual down a certain route, whether positive or negative. As a coach, your goal will be to lead them down a positive route. These types of questions can be helpful or manipulative, depending on how they are approached. Examples of leading questions and how they can be veered towards the negative or positive are as follows:

- "Are there any issues with taking on this project?"
- "Are you happy to take on this project?"

As you can see, the second question slightly leads a person towards the positive. Leading questions can also be used to coerce people into agreeing with a speaker. For example, a business coach can ask one of their clients, "This coaching session is going great, isn't it?" In a subtle way, the coach is almost forcing the client to answer in a certain way. A more appropriate question would be, "How are you feeling about this coaching session?" This is simple and unassuming.

A leading question can be used to build a positive discussion, which is good for a coaching session, or trying to steer the conversation towards an outcome that serves you, which is something you need to avoid in a coaching session. Avoid using leading questions as an unfair way to get what you want.

Loaded Questions

These questions are pretty straightforward and appear as closed questions, but come with a twist: They contain an assumption about the respondent. Some examples would be:

- Have you stopped drinking?
- Did you smoke your last cigarette this week?

- Are you going to revert back to your old habits?

Since the coaching and client relationship cannot work off of assumptions and finger-pointing, loaded questions should be avoided. Save these for when people are getting interrogated.

Funnel Questions

These questions begin broadly and then narrow up to a specific point, just like a funnel. They can also go in the opposite direction. When we meet someone new, we generally start with narrower questions and then broaden them out into more open-ended questions. For instance, you will ask someone their names during a first meeting and start asking broader questions to get more information.

In the reverse, broad questions are asked when more general information is needed and as we achieve it, we can slowly narrow things down to obtain more exact information. Funnel questions can be used to diffuse tension. For example, asking someone broad questions about an issue can distract them from their anger and gives you more information to help them find a solution.

Overall, funnel questions are great for developing relationships, discovering specific information, and diffusing arguments.

Rhetorical Questions

These types of questions don't really require an answer. They are more like phrases or statements disguised as questions so the conversation is more engaging for the listener. They can be used by coaches to get their clients to spur thoughts and ideas.

The Tone of a Question

In addition to the type of question to be asked, the tone is also important. This includes quality of voice, body language, and facial expressions. The tone of a question can completely alter the meaning, even if the same words are used. For example, a sarcastic tone will come off differently than a warm and friendly tone.

The matriculation of technology has thrown a wrench into the situation, as well. With the advent of emojis and gifs, new ways of reading messages have been born. As a coach, you always want to make sure you are conveying the right message with your tone. Always use techniques for clarification to make sure there are no misunderstandings.

6

TOP CORE BUSINESS COACHING SKILLS

Coaching has slowly risen to become a practice of helping people learn, but not telling them what to do. Instead, a coach helps people find the right answers within themselves which is where the best solutions come from. As a result of helping people make their own decisions, coaches can truly lead people into reaching their full potential.

A good coach will help their clients break down the barriers that are getting in their way. In most cases, the barrier is their own mind. The foundational belief in the coaching profession is that the client always has the answers to their problems, no matter how great they might be. They just need a little guidance along the way, and the coach can work as their roadmap or GPS. Therefore, the responsibility ultimately lies on the client, which means they can walk away knowing they have the capability to change their lives and that is very empowering.

Of course, this does not mean that the coach does not have any culpability. A good coach will know that they are responsible for making sure they give their best to their clients. A good coach never shows disinterest, assumes, judges, or dismisses their clients' feelings among other things. Most importantly coaches bring a certain set of skills to the table. These are part of their arsenal to give their clients the best of who they are.

COACHING SKILLS

Just because coaching is still largely an unregulated profession, does not mean you do not need excessive knowledge and training to be the best. You absolutely do because if you try to go in cold, you are setting yourself, and your clients, up for failure. This is definitely not fair to those who seek your help. The most important aspect of becoming a great business coach is the skills you develop to help others become the best versions of themselves.

The three core coaching skills are listening, thinking, and speaking. Coaches do these things differently than anyone else. When they listen, they try to really hear what the client is saying. What are their hopes and aspirations? What are their strengths and weaknesses? What are they really interested in? What things in life do they fear the most? What areas of their life is the client trying to avoid? Which aspects of their life do the clients seem fixated on? What is not being said during the session? Are there any inconsistencies in what the client is saying? A coaching session goes well beyond a regular discussion. The coach must actively listen for even the smallest clues that can lead the conversation into many different directions.

The next core is thinking. Thinking like a coach is much different than just thinking in the general sense. Coaches think in terms of now. Whatever happened in the past is not of great importance. Even if the coach and client relationship has been going on for a while, the main thing the coach has on their mind is what value they can bring to their client in that very moment they are with them, whether it is an actual session, a phone conference, or any other official interaction.

The final core skill is speaking. The way a coach speaks is also unique. When you are talking to someone in a conversation, their response to you is that of giving advice or their opinion. You are probably the same way when answering a person back. For a coach, speaking is done in the service of others. This means they do not speak to look good, feel good, or show how intelligent they are. The sole purpose of speaking is to serve their client.

While these are the core coaching skills, there are many more that we will get into while also providing greater details. Remember that without your coaching skills, you will not help your clients reach their potential. It is necessary to learn these methods for the sake of the clients you will work with in the future.

Listening

We touched upon the coaching skill of listening already but want to get into more depth because of how important it is. It is probably the most essential skill to possess as a coach because if you cannot listen well, you will not understand your client's needs and will not be able to respond appropriately. This is why we put this skill at the top of the list. This does not just mean listening to what is said, but what is not being said. A good coach must learn to read between the lines of a conversation. This is where some of the most important information is discovered.

This is where a coach can ask really insightful questions of their clients to determine what is going on. We discussed the GROW Model and how essential it is for asking appropriate questions. Always remember this technique when moving forward to get the most information about your client. Through the GROW Model, there are four levels of listening skills:

- Attentive listening: This is when you give someone your full attention without distractions or letting your mind wander. When someone is speaking to you, listen to them fully.
- Accurate listening: Completely understanding the issue at hand. If you do not understand it, then ask appropriate follow-up questions until you do.
- Empathetic listening: Listening and showing complete

appreciation of the person's feelings concerning the issue at hand. This is done without judgment. To listen empathetically, you must leave your own vantage point and put yourself in the other person's shoes.
- Generative listening: Once again, completely understanding the issues at hand which allows you to ask insightful questions based on what the person needs.

Questioning

After listening to someone appropriately, you must then be able to ask great questions which is at the heart of great coaching. There are so many types of questions we can use and we used numerous examples in chapter five. As you gain more experience as a coach, you will pick up on many more subtle clues that will lead you to ask specific questions.

Some questions are more helpful than others, even within the same coaching session, but the best ones give insight into who the client really is. Questions must be open-ended so that appropriate follow-up can be conducted at all times. In most cases, it takes multiple questions to find a real solution, so avoid asking anything that will close off a conversation immediately.

The best way to stick with open-ended questions is to think about the "5 Bums on a Rugby Post" method. Each bum makes the shape of a "W" and the rugby post has the "H" shape. For those of you who don't understand this reference, it means that each question should begin with one of the five "W" words: What, where, who, why, or when. Or, it can start with the "H" word, which is how. In a pure coaching scenario, only open-ended questions starting with these types of words are used.

One of the best tips for asking good questions is to play off your own curiosity. Be curious about your client and look at the process of gaining information as a treasure hunt. Do not stop asking questions until you find that magic solution or treasure. Once you do, ask some more.

Building Rapport

Chronologically speaking, this is the first skill you will need when you start working with any client in order for the relationship to move forward. In fact, you will need to build rapport beforehand because your clients need to trust you prior to working with you in the first place. If you do not create rapport right from the beginning, the remainder of the coaching process will not work. Even if a client chooses to be a part of some sessions, they will never open up fully. This will be a major problem in the long run.

The rapport should also be maintained throughout the relationships so the coach and client will continue to work well together. Rapport is what allows coachees to be relaxed and to become vulnerable. This is where the greatest truths are revealed and personal barriers and fears are identified. Having good rapport also allows the coach to ask more difficult and insightful questions.

Some of the key factors in creating rapport include:

- Having empathy, or the ability to see the other person's point of view. We will get into more detail about this later.
- Having the right body language portrays a welcoming tone. For example, it is better to sit forward in a chair and look like you're attuned with the client, than sitting with our back against a chair with your arms folded. The latter will make it seem like you are not engaged whatsoever. You can also match and mirror your client's body language.
- Being warm and personable. Instead of sitting right across from someone, sit at more of an angle.
- Using the right tone of voice and language.

It is easier to build rapport with someone who appears honest and interested from the beginning. An important thing to note is that the coaching and client connection is similar to other types of relationships in that you will not always click with everybody. For whatever reason, you will not be able to coach certain people, not because you aren't good at it, but because the dynamics are not compatible. Sometimes, two people are like oil and water and there is nothing that can be done about it.

Always give it the college try and put in your best effort as a coach. However, when it becomes apparent that progress is not being made, it is better to cut things off respectfully and go in separate directions. If possible, you can certainly assist the client in finding a more compatible coach.

Having a good rapport with clients leads directly to successful coaching sessions.

Rapport

Empathizing

Empathy is defined as the ability to put ourselves in other people's shoes so we can get a perspective from their point of view. Often, it is hard to imagine why someone would make certain decisions or think a particular way. When we show empathy, we are more likely to appreciate their feelings and behavior in any given situation. As a coach, you will understand what it feels like to be your client.

Empathy is one of the most important people skills to have. It is essential for good communication and to remember that our focus should not be on what we would do in a situation, but what is best for that particular person to do. Empathy is such a forgotten skill because people are overly focused on themselves.

The goal of empathy is to help you understand the needs of another person. This is exceptionally important when building rapport in a coaching relationship. The client must feel like you are trying to understand them. When they realize this, they will be much more forthcoming with their personal information.

Empathy is often confused with sympathy, but it is not the same thing. Sympathy is simply feeling compassion for the hardship a person is going through, whereas empathy means you become one with the person going through the distress. Sometimes, you can actually feel what they feel during the most extreme forms of empathy. Both of these qualities are great to have in the coaching profession but empathy definitely takes it a step further.

Summarizing and Reflecting

These two skills help guide your client in making sense of what they are grappling with. Summarizing means you are repeating a condensed version of what the client said. With this process, you take the main point of their message and reiterate them. This will allow the client to make any corrections about what was understood by the coach and make sure everyone is on the same page. In addition, summarizing keeps the client focused on the topic at hand so continued progress can be made. As a coach, it's important to use this summarizing technique to reduce any chances of miscommunication. If you are unsure of what the client said, don't hesitate to ask them as many follow-up questions as needed.

Reflecting is another strategy where the coach paraphrases what their coachee said in order to show comprehension. This is an effective skill that can reinforce the thoughts of the client. The coach will also be able to step back and look at what was said objectively. Both of these techniques will ensure proper and clear communication is taking place between the coach and client.

Unlocking Limiting Beliefs

Many clients that you work with have not realized their goals because they do not believe in themselves enough. They are halted by their limiting beliefs and you have the opportunity to help them overcome these barriers of the mind. Beliefs are a principle that is automatically accepted as true without any real proof. Therefore, a person who believes they are not good enough, smart enough, or talented enough has a mindset that's not rooted in any facts. The only reason they have limiting beliefs is that they are too hard on themselves. Perhaps past failures are plaguing their mind, but the past should not predict the future.

Our beliefs have a significant impact on our behavior, which ultimately decide our results. Some beliefs make us successful, while others hold us back. Limiting beliefs can make people feel trapped. Where do these limitations come from, there can be a variety of sources, like past failures, the environment, how people were treated as children, and the support system they have now.

As a coach, helping your clients identify the underlying causes of their limiting beliefs and then challenge them is one of the most powerful coaching processes there can be. This process can be extremely emotional and enlightening for the client, and you, as the coach, will play a major role. Once again, you are not telling them what their limiting beliefs are, but guiding them into finding their own answers and solutions. Your role will be to get the other person to question their inner beliefs. It might be something they have never done before, so expect a little bit of pushback. However, if you have built up some rapport as we discussed earlier, you will have a better chance of getting through.

Staying Focused

When we are just talking in general conversation, it is not unusual to veer off track and discuss many different topics. During a session, it is important for a coach to make sure everything stays on track. The conversation must be focused on finding answers to the client's particular problems and not degenerate into just a regular discussion. Also, do not digress by getting into too much detail. We are not saying you can't be friendly and have some fun with your client, but do not lose sight of the goal.

To remain focused, you can use many of the techniques already described, like the GROW Model, asking appropriate questions, and summarizing. You may also need to interject once in a while to pull the conversation back to the center. Allow your client the freedom to express themselves, but do not allow them to completely go off the rails. There are still problems that need solutions.

Being Non-Judgemental and Open-Minded

When you judge someone, you have already made up your mind about who they are and what they are capable of. A coach is supposed to help their clients realize their own potential and live without limits. This is why it's critical to be non-judgemental. As a coach, you do not get to judge another human being. You must maintain your curiosity and remain open-minded to all of the possibilities the client will come up with. Being open-minded means being empathetic too. This gives you the ability to view the world through their prism. From their vantage point, their views may be the right ones for them.

Open-minded

Resisting the Temptation to Tell

Being a coach is different than being a consultant or mentor. This is why you must never tell the client what to think. It can be very tempting to do so because humans like to solve other people's problems. It makes them feel good. However, that is not the purpose of coaching. The client has the best outcomes and will remain accountable when they are allowed to come up with their own solutions. In the end, they will appreciate it more too. Always resist the temptation to tell or give advice.

Give Constructive Feedback

The great thing about being a coach is that you can provide an outside perspective for someone that is objective since you don't have a personal connection. As a coach, you will be in a privileged position to point out certain things you notice about your clients, like their behaviors, facial expressions, reactions to specific questions, or body language during certain moments. Of course, keep these observations non-judgemental. For example, you can simply point out that they smile when certain words are spoken and become closed off with other words.

In most cases, your feedback will be well received by your client, especially if you have developed a rapport. It is pretty apparent that not much can be accomplished without rapport from the beginning. When you are giving feedback, make sure it is the following:

- Motivating
- Honest and from the heart
- Empathetic
- Timely
- Specific
- Balanced
- Actionable

There is a major difference between feedback and criticism. Do not tell a person something just for the heck of it. Point it out should be helpful to them in some way.

There are many coaching skills that you must develop before you are able to help your clients. They will seek you out for help, so you must do as much as you can to guide them towards success. Clients will have many fears and concerns when they are going into business. Having a good relationship with a business can make all the difference in the world.

INCREASING EMPATHY

Since empathy is such an important skill to have in order to really put your clients first, We will discuss some action steps you can take to increase your empathy. With empathy, you are able to understand another person's feelings and emotions because you are partly sharing them. You can feel what they are going through, which makes you more helpful in guiding them towards solutions. People who lack empathy are viewed as cold, self-absorbed, and uncaring. To become a good coach, you want to avoid getting this type of reputation. Remember that a client can only know what you show them. If you show them disinterest, whether it's true or not, then they will never be fully vulnerable with you.

Empathy is partly innate and partly learned. This means that some people are naturally more empathetic, while others are trained to be over time. Whatever the case, you can become more empathetic through certain action steps. We will go over those here.

Challenge Yourself

Many times, people become non-empathetic because they don't remember, or ever knew, what it was like to experience discomfort. If you challenge yourself by going out of your comfort zone, you will start understanding what it's like to be in an uncomfortable setting, like so many people are. It makes you less soft.

To challenge yourself, you can do something out of the ordinary every day, like going to a new restaurant or trying an activity you've never done before. You can take courses to increase your skillset, like learning a new language, taking an art class, or signing up for training at a local college. You can also do something more daring, like skydiving or bungee-jumping if you are willing to.

Doing things to get you out of your comfort zone will humble you, and humility is one of the main enablers of empathy.

Get Out of Your Usual Environment

Do you believe that the rest of the world thinks just like you do? Are you unaware of the many cultures that exist out there? If so, it is time for you to get out of your familiar environment. You don't have to travel abroad even though that is an option. Just go somewhere you have never been before, even if that place is just a few towns over. Being in a different setting will give you a new perspective you've never had before. By doing this, you will develop a greater appreciation for other people. You will soon realize that not everyone lives and thinks like you, and this can be very enlightening. You will soon learn that another person will view the world from a different lens. This realization is also important for empathy to occur.

Get Feedback

Ask for feedback from people who know you well, like friends, family, or colleagues. Have them give you their opinions on the various skills you possess, like listening, asking questions, body language, facial expression, and other communication factors. Ask for feedback frequently so you stay sharp.

Explore the Heart, Not Just the Head

A technique that many medical schools use to increase empathy in their future doctors is to have them read literature that explores emotions and personal relationships. This strategy makes people realize that other people have specific emotions and feelings during certain situations, and they may be vastly different from your own. This is a simple trick you can start using, especially if you love to read. Another option is watching emotional movies or TV shows.

Walk in Other People's Shoes

We don't mean this literally, but you can ask other people what it is like to live in their current situation. What moods are they going through and why? What is the underlying reason behind this and are their specific triggers? Slowly but surely, this technique will teach you about other people's experiences and how they perceived similar experiences as you went through. Once you start walking to people about how they felt during certain moments that you also went through, you begin learning how the viewpoints of some people are drastically different than yours. You will begin understanding that not everyone thinks or reacts like you and they're not necessarily wrong in doing that.

. . .

Examine Your Biases

We all have biases that prevent us from being fully empathetic. Biases are judgments we are making towards a person without having much knowledge of the situation. For example, if we see someone who is overweight, we might assume they are lazy and don't take care of themselves. We don't take into account that there could be certain factors beyond their control. It is important to examine your biases and assess how they are causing you to jump to conclusions. If you don't think you have any biases, think again. Sometimes, they become so ingrained in us that we don't realize they are there.

Cultivate Your Sense of Curiosity

We have already described this as an essential coaching skill and it is a great way to develop empathy. What can you learn from a new employee who comes into your office? What can you learn from your child? What can you learn from your client? Curious people ask a lot of questions and follow up questions too until they arrive at an answer. You will do this with your clients too, which will naturally boost your empathy. Oh, and asking good questions is the final action step we are going to mention towards improving empathy.

7

LEADERSHIP DEVELOPMENT COACH

"Leadership is about making others better as a result of your presence and making sure that impact lasts in your absence."

— SHERYL SANBERG, COO OF FACEBOOK

A leader is anyone who has the responsibility of managing a group. There can be many different variations of leaders. Most people think of CEOs, high-level executives, or business-owners as leaders. Managers and supervisors can also be placed in this category. A leader can be a person who is heading up a particular group project. Heads of households, like parents or guardians, can be considered leaders, as well.

Being a leader is not so much about having a title, but how you conduct yourself. Leaders are those who command attention and respect through words and actions. Leaders will often rise to the top of any situation and will often step forward to accept challenges, while others step back. A leader is able to inspire others to be their best selves. Finally, they are the ones people look to for guidance, whether they are in a leadership role or not. Their presence is attractive to people.

While true leaders don't always have to be in an official role, most of them naturally shift towards these positions because of how they carry themselves. In times of crisis, people look towards a strong leader. This is why they must be taken care of too.

"People who are truly strong lift others up. People who are truly powerful bring others together."

— MICHELLE OBAMA

Leadership

LEADERSHIP DEVELOPMENT COACHING

Who is guiding these leaders to become the best versions of themselves? Oftentimes, it is a leadership development coach, which is a sector of business coaching that we will discuss here. Having good leaders is essential in our society, but too many of them take the wrong approach when it comes to actual leadership. After a while, the people they are leading can start to lose faith and stop following directions. The members of a group may even start blaming their leader for failures they have personally encountered.

Leadership development coaches are there to guide leadership clients in developing their essential qualities. These types of coaches can help leaders understand their shortcomings in order to correct them. The relationship is a collaborative effort to achieve a set goal. The overall objective is to transform the quality of a leader's work and personal life.

Leadership development coaching:

- Improves the skills and knowledge of their clients.
- Provides a foundation for better work-life balance.
- Works to develop higher emotional intelligence.
- Helps leaders at the interpersonal and organizational levels.

Leadership development coaching is many things, but here's what it's not:

- Technical guidance
- Consulting
- Career counseling
- Job training

It is simply a partnership that helps leaders accomplish short-term and long-term organizational goals.

BENEFITS OF LEADERSHIP DEVELOPMENT COACHING

Leadership development has some interesting benefits to consider.

Flow-on Effect

This type of coaching leads to effective leaders and healthier organizations. As leaders are able to improve their skills, the positive benefits will spread across the entire organization.

Leaders in any sector are the ones who set the tone for whatever environment they are in. So, if they can show strength through their emotions, it will have an impact on everyone around them. Senior leaders who are exposed to leadership development coaching develop a flow-on effect, which creates a new coaching culture within an organization.

Leaders learn new skills through an effective coaching process and pass them on to those who follow them. This results in improved performance, productivity, and better outcomes. Creating a coaching environment leads to space where people will be empathetic, understanding, patient, and helpful to one another just like any coach would be.

Personalized Attention

As many more organizations are looking to operate at peak performance, coaching is becoming a viable option to get them there. Many businesses go the route of seminars, workshops, and other training programs. However, these options are very generalized with the same information for all groups. Coaching is much more targeted and tailored towards a particular person or organization's needs. This personal attention is what makes the field of coaching so attractive.

Coaches use their training and skills to analyze each individual and help them explore their full potential. The process of coaching challenges clients in a way they've never been before and forces them out of their comfort zone. They realize that many of the beliefs they had their whole lives are not as real as they once thought. After working with a coach, business clients will begin welcoming change, which is needed for growth.

Personalized attention

SKILLS NEEDED FOR LEADERSHIP DEVELOPMENT COACHING

Just like any other type of coaching, leadership development coaching requires a proper skill set. You cannot become a hirable coach without these attributes. Let's go over some of them.

Communication Skills

This is pretty much a given, but in order to be a great coach, you need to be a great communicator. This does just not mean you are good at talking. It encompasses all aspects of communications. You will get a wide variety of clients throughout your career who come from different backgrounds, cultures, and socioeconomic statuses. Some individuals will be extroverts, while others will be introverts. You will need to learn how to communicate well with all of them.

As a coach, you must encourage people to tell their side of the story and then listen actively to what they say. You need to be able to pick up on clues and ask good follow up questions, summarize, and reflect on what they said. Poor communication will result in a lot of misunderstandings. Make sure the messages going both ways are as crisp and clear as possible.

Always keep in mind that your tone, body language, and attitude matter, as well. It's what just what you say, but how you say it, and when you say it. You will have many challenging clients who will test your patience. You must not lose your cool. Take any criticism and resistance in a positive way by always responding with gentleness. Using proper communication methods will help ease your client's tension. Think of yourself as a leader during a coaching session and act as a leader would.

Influencing and Negotiation Skills

The best leadership development coaches do not command authority. They do not boss people around or control them in any way. Instead, they inspire and encourage others. Just like any coach and client relationship, it is a collaboration between two people trying to learn more about the coachee.

Great leaders know that influence matters much more than power. They know how to negotiate a deal so it's not all one-sided, but a win-win for all who are involved. As a leadership development coach, you must practice what you preach. Before you can help your clients develop their leadership skills, you must have them yourself.

Negotiating

Conflict Management Skills

There are some people in this world who are always ready for conflict and will create it whenever they can. Sometimes, conflict just arises out of nowhere. As a coach, you will have clients like this and they will be difficult to manage. Some of them will be short-tempered while others will be in situations that will make them act this way. Some clients will have no hope and resist the coaching process heavily. Finally, some of your clients will blame you for their failures. There is the potential for many different conflicts to arise so you must be able to manage it as a coach.

As a leadership development coach, you will have two main advantages in regards to conflict management skills:

- It will help in your coaching process.
- You will set a great example for your client. They will learn to manage and resolve conflicts by taking inspiration from you.

By displaying conflict management skills, your client will become a better leader.

Change Management Skills

A coaching session will never be predictable and you never know when you will need to change things up. You may have had a strong plan going in, but that can change at the drop of a hat. As you proceed with the coaching sessions with your clients, you will experience many changes.

In addition, there will be many difficult situations that you will face, and there is a possibility that you will not get clients right away. You need to have change management skills in order to deal with unpredictable situations.

Questioning and Listening Skills

Questioning and listening are the best ways to understand the situation your client is currently in. We have already gone over asking appropriate questions and listening skills but just wanted to reiterate their importance here. Never be in a rush to get to the next question.

. . .

Analyzing Skills

Once you have identified the points of pain for a client, the next step is to analyze them thoroughly. The following are some questions you can ask:

- What is the cause of the pain?
- What options are available for you?
- What potential alternatives exist?
- What strengths and weaknesses do you possess?
- What should you focus on to transform into the leader you want to be?

Analyze the current situation thoroughly while also having the end goal in mind.

PRINCIPLES OF LEADERSHIP DEVELOPMENT COACHING

Along with the coaching skills, there are specific principles involved in leadership development coaching that you must also be aware of. These principles will guide your coaching process if you incorporate them into your practice.

Align With the Coachee's Agenda

The cardinal rule of coaching is that it must be client-focused and never about you as the coach. Your goal is to do what's best for your client, so you must put your ego aside and become humble. Therefore, never tell the coachee what they should be focused on or what needs to be the priority in their lives. They need to figure this out on their own. You can guide them as needed, but do not impose your will in any way on them.

A leadership development coach simply helps their client discover the answers they already have within them.

Collaborate

The leadership development coach should only act as a collaborator in assisting their clients, but the coachee has the ultimate say. In fact, a coach should not really sway their decision one way or another. They can just help facilitate the transition.

Advocate Self-Awareness

Self-awareness means having a conscious knowledge of one's current status, characters, desires, feelings, and motives. A good leader should always be self-aware of their particular strengths and weaknesses. Exhibit a sense of self-awareness within yourself and your client will foster something similar within themselves. Once again, you can lead by example.

Always model the leadership qualities that you try to instill in your clients. Practice what you preach and your clients will have greater faith in knowing what you are talking about.

WHY HIRE A LEADERSHIP DEVELOPMENT COACH

If you are not already convinced about the benefits of leadership development coaching or the coaching practice in general, then continue reading to fully recognize why someone would hire a coach in this regard. If you want to explain to potential clients why they should hire you, the following reasons are a great start.

Empowerment

Leadership development coaches can empower their clients to become powerful leaders and do exceptional work. Through the use of several coaching tools and techniques, you can help a client discover their full potential. You can get them to think in a way they never have before. The relationship a client has with their coach will help them achieve some much-needed transformation to vastly change their circumstances.

Fresh Insight

Leaders can gain some fresh perspective from their coach. During times of great stress and feeling overwhelmed a client may not be able to see things clearly. The coach can help them sit back and reflect on their situation. The coach can analyze what is happening through a different lens and find deeper problems. From here, the coach can build a plan to tackle similar problems in the future.

Free Thinking

Coaches will allow free-thinking in their clients. Many people are in structured environments where they must think a certain way or think very quickly to get the job done. During a coaching session, the client actually has some time to reflect. They can also consider different thought patterns and views. Free thinking encourages flexible leadership, which is important for decision-making.

Enhanced Performance

The leadership development coaching process makes a huge difference in someone's attitude and abilities. Coaches help their clients learn and put in place new techniques. These strategies are tailored around clients' weaknesses and help them avoid self-defeating words, like "but," "maybe," or "yet." A leadership development coach will help transform the personality of a leader to make them stronger in their field. The transformation alone is worth the investment in coaching.

BUSINESS/LIFE BALANCE

Now that we have covered business coaching in great detail, we will go over some ways a coach can help their clients set up a work/life balance. Or in our case, business/life balance. This is something that will become part of your skillset as a coach. The purpose of running a business is to have autonomy so you have some freedom to run your life. If you are working all the time, that reason becomes moot.

Whether you are a small business owner or run a large corporation, a big chunk of your life will be dedicated to your business. The hours are long and the rewards are few at the very beginning. While being a business owner does ask a lot of someone, you must never lose sight of the fact that you have a personal life.

As a business coach, you will be running your own business too, so maintaining work/life balance is important for you, as well. This is another opportunity for you to be an example for your client. Once you develop the skills to maintain balance in your life, you can impart your knowledge to your client. As always, your goal will be to guide them towards their own path. We will no go over some ways to create and sustain a balance between business and personal life.

Get Help

Business owners, especially when they are new, have a tendency to take on a lot of responsibility on their own. Normally, this is the work of multiple people being done by one individual. If you are going to maintain work/life balance, you cannot expect to do it all on your own and not work 24/7.

Consider hiring people to help you with certain tasks and projects. As a business coach, you can help your client figure out what areas of their business can be done by other people so they have the time to focus on more important items that require more of their attention. If you don't want to hire full-time employees, you can hire independent contractors.

Set a Schedule

If you want to get everything done, you must set a schedule that will structure your day into specific blocks. For example, you can block off specific hours of the days for certain business-related items while also setting aside time blocks for fun and relaxation. Once you set up your schedule, stick to the times as much as possible.

As a business coach, you can assist your client in creating a proper schedule that will work well for their needs. When the day is structured and you have a plan, it is much easier to find time to do the things you want to do.

Prioritize

To balance your life properly, you need to prioritize what is important to you. Always put your most important tasks first and get them over with. That way, if you need to push anything back, it will be your less urgent items on the list. When you are setting your priorities, make self-care one of them. Block off time for self-care and stick to these times as much as possible.

Take Breaks

You cannot run around all day at work without sitting down or taking a break. You will burn out and be unable to function in other areas of your life. Carve out time every day whether you are at work or home.

Get a Hobby

When you run a business of any kind, it is nearly impossible to completely separate your business life from your personal life. This is just the nature of the entrepreneur beast. To help combat this, find a hobby that is completely separate from work and something you will never mix in with your business. Once you have your hobby, set aside time for it every week.

Take Time Off

When you are running your own business, we know it can seem impossible to just take time off. After all, when you are not open, you are not making money. If you are working seven days a week, spending some quality time to yourself at the end of every day is not enough. You need more time than this. Try to take at least one day off in a week to get away from your business. As a coach, you can help your client explore which day of the week is generally the slowest on average and encourage the client to take that particular day off every week. It's worth a shot to get some relaxation.

Set Boundaries

Since you cannot separate your business life and personal life completely, you can at least set some boundaries. When you are doing stuff for your business, try to keep your personal life out of it. When you are at home, try to avoid bringing your business issues into it. You can also make rules that you will not do any business-related activities after a certain time. Whatever you can do to maintain a boundary, do it.

Find Your Productivity

Get the most out of your workday by finding your productivity. The more productive you are, the more tasks you will get done within a specific time period which means more of your personal time will remain your personal time.

Stay Connected

A major part of having a personal life is staying connected with other people. Healthy relationships that are not work-related are essential for maintaining balance. Stay involved with your friends, make time to spend with them, be an active member of your community, and spend whatever time you can away from the demands of your business.

As you can see, the strategies we covered throughout this book will help to create a positive work/life balance. Be that example for your clients and improve your work/life balance.

CONCLUSION

We had a great time writing this book, *Who Wants to Be a Superhero If You Can be a Business Coach?* All of us at Elvin Coaches want to thank you for taking the time to read it. We hope that you are as excited about learning business coaching as we are talking about it. Coaching is a powerful industry that can change people's lives in an instant. In fact, it has been for many decades now and all of us have seen this happen personally.

Business coaching is a major sector of the larger life coaching industry where the focus is to help clients build their business no matter what state they are in. Whether someone is just thinking about transitioning into the business world, is actively opening up their first business, or has been successful in business for years, they can all benefit heavily from a business coach.

Business coaching utilizes effective techniques, the most common ones being asking appropriate questions and listening with intent. These methods help guide business clients to find the best solutions to their problems. Like any other type of life coach, a business coach will never tell a client what to do but will help them explore the answers that are already inside of them. This is where the best solutions are found. When someone is able to figure things out on their own, it is a big boost to their self-confidence. Coaching works from the assumption that all people are capable of solving their problems, they just need some direction along the way.

After reading this book, we anticipate that you have a thorough understanding of what business coaching is, what benefits it can have for entrepreneurs, and the steps you can take to become one yourself if you desire to do so. Our hope is that you gained an interest in this field and will decide to partake in it in the future. We love the coaching industry and want as many talented people to join our profession.

In this book, we also covered the various sunsets of business coaching, like leadership development coaching and time management coaching. If you can find a good specialty that interests you within the business coaching field, you will be able to work with a niche market and provide in-depth help towards a targeted group.

Marketing is something you cannot forget about, whether you are the coach or the client. This means that you must take advantage of effective marketing strategies in your coaching business and guide your clients in proper advertising methods for their own venture, whatever it may be. No matter how good a product, service, or idea is, no one will know it exists if the marketing is not done properly. The advertising and marketing industries are changing and innovating constantly. Staying up to date on the newest trends is essential for optimal success.

Despite what area of business coaching you get into, many of the same principles for success will apply. Of course, each sector will have their own unique methods as well. Overall, before you get into business coaching on your own, fully understand the role you will play and the strategies you need to help your clients to the best of your ability. It is advisable to hire a business coach of your own to help make the transition smooth. The focus of any coaching session is the client that needs help. A coach should use these opportunities to provide as much value to their coachee as possible, and not worry about their ego or reputation. A reputation will be built once the clients start spreading the word about your coaching strategies. Give them something good to talk about.

Once you become a business coach and attract multiple clients, you will be your own boss and will benefit from the freedom of being an entrepreneur. Of course, the classic joke here is that an entrepreneur will work eighty hours a week for themselves to avoid working forty hours a week for someone else. There is definitely an element of truth to this statement. However, working for yourself still gives you a sense of freedom despite how many hours you may be working.

Along with guiding their clients towards successful business practices, coaches will also help their clients develop a work/life balance. Business owners will put in many hours and it is impossible to completely separate work issues from personal matters. At some point, one area will bleed into the other and vice versa. Of course, this does not mean that certain practices cannot be put in place to limit the crossover between business and home life. With the amount of stress owning a business can create, it is essential to break away regularly to decompress and re-energize.

Business coaching is a dynamic field and all of us at Elvin Coaches are excited that you got a taste of what the coaching industry is all about. We say taste because the field encompasses so much, and you must experience it first hand to understand what it entails.

If you are excited about what you've read so far and want to experience business coaching first hand, do not wait any longer. Do your research about coaches in your area and try out a few sessions. We expect that you are involved, or plan to be involved, in some type of business. After experiencing the benefits of coaching, you can work on becoming a business coach yourself, if that is your goal. The prospects are great and the industry, as a whole, is growing exponentially. As more people realize the value of coaching, it will continue to grow and pros-

CONCLUSION | 155

per. We are confident that once you start participating in the coaching practice, both as a client and coach, you will never look back.

Finally, we want as many people as possible to learn about the field of business coaching. If you found the information to be valuable, a positive review would be greatly appreciated so more people can learn about this book and benefit from it. Thank you again for taking the time to read it.

Freedom

PLEASE LEAVE A REVIEW

Did you enjoy the book??

Reviews are the life blood of an author. If you can please take a few minutes to leave a review.

Even a short review helps, like "Great book!".

Just for you!

A FREE GIFT TO OUR READERS

Scan the QR code to subscribe or follow the link
https://elvinlifecoaches.activehosted.com/f/3

You're going to receive the

Wheel of Life Coaching Technique

and other goodies

REFERENCES

18 Examples of Bad Coaching Habits. (2016, May 10). Center for Executive Coaching. https://www.centerforexecutivecoaching.com/articles/bad-coaching-habits/

Achieving Work-Life Balance as a Small Business Owner. (2020, February 4). Ama La Vida. https://alvcoaching.com/work-life-balance-small-business-owner/

Blackbyrn, Sai. "Become An Amazing Leadership Development Coach In 2020 - .Coach." *..Coach*, .Coach Blog, 20 June 2020, sai.coach/blog/leadership-development-coach-2020/. Accessed 8 Oct. 2020.

Blackbyrn, Sai. "How To Become The Best Marketing Coach In 2020 - .Coach." *..Coach*, .Coach Blog, 3 Mar. 2020, sai.coach/blog/marketing-coach-2020/. Accessed 9 Oct. 2020.

REFERENCES

Bluepoint Leadership Development. "The Three Core Coaching Skills." *YouTube*, 27 Aug. 2013, www.youtube.com/watch?v=bYZZQigqZQs. Accessed 6 Oct. 2020.

Boolkah, P. (2017). What Does A Business Coach Do? | The Benefits Of Coaching And Mentoring For Business Owners [YouTube Video]. In *YouTube*. https://www.youtube.com/watch?v=BqLhT8hJpuQ

Breakingpic. (n.d.). *Green Note Card and Four Scrabble Tiles on Gray Surface*. Retrieved October 8, 2020, from https://www.pexels.com/photo/postit-scrabble-to-do-todo-3299/

Burrows, Kate. "Coaching Skills | Ultimate Guide | Coaching Techniques." *Making Business Matter*, 3 Apr. 2018, www.makingbusinessmatter.co.uk/coaching-skills-ultimate-guide/#10. Accessed 9 Oct. 2020.

Cabello, A. (n.d.). *Man Blindfolded*. Retrieved October 9, 2020, from https://www.pexels.com/photo/man-blindfolded-1278620/

Christian, L. (2019, July 9). *What is a Business Coach (and Are They Effective in 2020)?* SoulSalt. https://soulsalt.com/what-is-a-business-coach/

Chuangch, A. (n.d.). *Black Analog Alarm Clock at 7:01*. Retrieved October 6, 2020, from https://www.pexels.com/photo/accurate-alarm-alarm-clock-analogue-359989/

Duczeminski, Matt. "5 Reasons to Embrace Vulnerability." *Lifehack*, 19 June 2015, www.lifehack.org/273700/5-reasons-embrace-vulnerability. Accessed 9 Oct. 2020.

Fauxels. (n.d.-b). *Photo of People Near Wooden Table*. Retrieved October 6, 2020, from https://www.pexels.com/photo/photo-of-people-near-wooden-table-3184418/

Fewtrell, B. (2019, July 11). *Build & Grow your Business with MaxMyProfit*. MaxMyProfit. https://maxmyprofit.com.au/blog/7-step-guide-to-becoming-a-business-coach/

Foo, S. (2020, May 4). *Blogging As Your Marketing Tool: How It Works & Why To Start*. SpeechSilver. https://speechsilver.com/blogging-as-your-marketing-tool/

Forbes Coaches Council. (2018, January 25). *Council Post: 15 Effective Ways To Establish Credibility As A Business Coach*. Forbes. https://www.forbes.com/sites/forbescoachescouncil/2018/01/25/15-effective-ways-to-establish-credibility-as-a-business-coach/#3689c73ad23b

Guthrie, G. (2018, October 24). *8 Essential Questioning Techniques You Need to Know*. Typetalk. https://www.typetalk.com/blog/the-8-essential-questioning-techniques-you-need-to-know/

Pixabay. (n.d.-h). *Group of People Holding Arms*. Retrieved October 8, 2020, from https://www.pexels.com/photo/ground-group-growth-hands-461049/

Juhaszimrus, S. (n.d.). *123 Let's Go Imaginary Text*. Retrieved October 8, 2020, from https://www.pexels.com/photo/123-lets-go-imaginary-text-704767/

Kaboompics.com. (n.d.). *Customers & Users/Color Wheel*. Retrieved October 8, 2020, from https://www.pexels.com/photo/customers-users-color-wheel-6231/

Komar, Marlen. "7 Ways To Let Yourself Become More Vulnerable." *Bustle*, 28 Mar. 2016, www.bustle.com/articles/150219-7-ways-to-let-yourself-become-more-vulnerable. Accessed 9 Oct. 2020.

Lui, E. (n.d.). *Signboard with Time is Precious title on black background*. Retrieved October 8, 2020, from https://www.pexels.com/photo/signboard-with-time-is-precious-title-on-black-background-4151043/

Magni, O. (n.d.). *Person Resting Their Hand on Table*. Retrieved October 8, 2020, from https://www.pexels.com/photo/person-resting-their-hand-on-table-2058147/

Mazumder, A. (n.d.). *Person Holding a Green Plant*. Retrieved October 8, 2020, from https://www.pexels.com/photo/person-holding-a-green-plant-1072824/

McCarthy, Dan. "70 Coaching Questions for Managers Using the GROW Model." *The Balance Careers*, 19 Nov. 2019, www.thebalancecareers.com/coaching-questions-for-managers-2275913. Accessed 9 Oct. 2020.

Miller, Dan. "7 Reasons I Love Being a Coach." *Official Site Dan Miller*, 30 June 2015, www.48days.com/7-reasons-i-love-being-a-coach/. Accessed 9 Oct. 2020.

Mind Tools Content Team. (2009b). *How Can I Stop Procrastinating?Overcoming the Habit of Delaying Important Tasks*. Mindtools.Com. https://www.mindtools.com/pages/article/newHTE_96.htm

Mindvalley. (n.d.-b). *Ultimate Guide To Becoming a Business Coach*. Evercoach - By Mindvalley. Retrieved October 2, 2020, from https://www.evercoach.com/ultimate-guide-to-becoming-a-business-coach

Newlands, M. (2015, January 9). *10 Simple Steps to Improve Productivity*. Inc.Com. https://www.inc.com/murray-newlands/10-simple-steps-to-improve-productivity.html

Pixabay. (n.d.-l). *Questions Answers Signage*. Retrieved October 8, 2020, from https://www.pexels.com/photo/questions-answers-signage-208494/

Pixabay. (n.d.-l). *Red and Yellow Hatchback Axa Crash Tests*. Retrieved October 8, 2020, from https://www.pexels.com/photo/red-and-yellow-hatchback-axa-crash-tests-163016/

Roseclay, D. (n.d.). *Brown Framed Eyeglasses*. Retrieved October 9, 2020, from https://www.pexels.com/photo/brown-framed-eyeglasses-905163/

Scott, S. J. (2016, January 19). *How to Form a New Habit (in 8 Easy Steps)*. Develop Good Habits. https://www.developgoodhabits.com/how-to-form-a-habit-in-8-easy-steps/

Sobel, A. (2016). *Eight Ways to Improve Your Empathy*. Andrewsobel.Com. https://andrewsobel.com/eight-ways-to-improve-your-empathy/

Spiske, M. (n.d.). Retrieved October 8, 2020, from https://www.pexels.com/photo/crowd-reflection-color-toy-1679618/

Stavrinos, S. (n.d.). *Monochrome Photography of People Shaking Hands*. Retrieved October 6, 2020, from https://www.pexels.com/photo/monochrome-photography-of-people-shaking-hands-814544/

Tang, Cham. "The 4 Marketing Fundamentals." *Authentic Education*, 2 Feb. 2018, www.authentic.com.au/blog/marketing/4-marketing-fundamentals/. Accessed 9 Oct. 2020.

Thanyakij, B. (n.d.). *Person Writing on White Paper*. Retrieved October 8, 2020, from https://www.pexels.com/photo/person-writing-on-white-paper-3815585/

Timely Blog. "5 Essential Time Management Techniques – Timely Blog." *Memory*, 27 Aug. 2020, memory.ai/timely-blog/time-management-techniques. Accessed 9 Oct. 2020.

Wade, Francis. "How to Make a Difference as a Time Management Coach." *Lifehack*, 2 May 2012, www.lifehack.org/articles/productivity/how-to-make-a-difference-as-a-time-management-coach.html. Accessed 9 Oct. 2020.

Winkler, M. (n.d.-b). *Green Typewriter on Brown Wooden Table*. Retrieved October 6, 2020, from https://www.pexels.com/photo/green-typewriter-on-brown-wooden-table-4052198/